Susan M. Schultz

MEDITATIONS

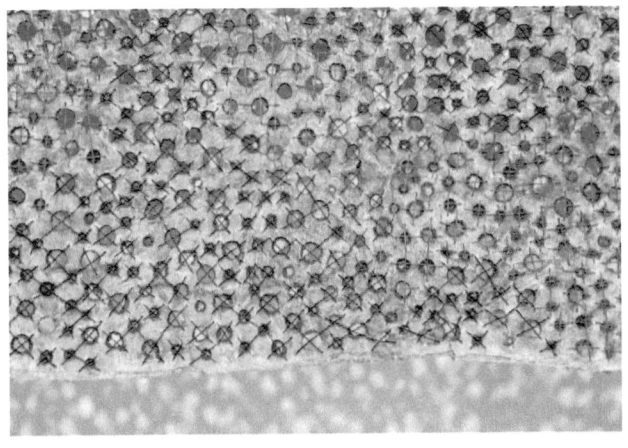

December 2019 – December 2020

Lyrical Prose

Wet Cement Press
Berkeley, Asheville, Reno

Meditations: December 2019–December 2020
©2023 by Susan M. Schultz

ISBN: 979-8-9883840-3-8

Library of Congress Control Number: 2023941932

Cover image:
Detail from "wasted (ii)" by Deborah G. Nehmad
Honolulu Museum of Art. Gift of the artist
in honor of James F. Jensen, 2017 (2017-1-02)

Published by Wet Cement Press

Wet Cement Press

1908 Yolo Ave
Berkeley, CA 94707

www.wetcementpress.com

Acknowledgments

Some of these meditations first appeared (with numbers that no longer apply) in *Chant de la Sirène, Court Green, Golden Handcuffs Review, Marsh Hawk Review, Saginaw, Unlikely Stories, Writing Out of Time Blog.* Thank you to the editors: Laura Hinton, Tony Trigilio, Lou Rowan, Eileen Tabios, David Harrison Horton, Jonathan Penton, Joe Harrington, Jennifer Dick and Carla Billitteri. And to Ed Foster for his kind support.

Thanks also to Deborah G. Nehmad for the use of the detail from her painting, "wasted (ii)."

Thank you to my immediate family: Anne, Bryant, Sangha, Radhika, Lilith, Thurney, Maeve, and Claude. And to everyone who read blog versions along the way, as well as to my students.

For my poetry sangha:
Hank Lazer, Norman Fischer, Lissa Wolsak,
Gillian Parrish, Paul Naylor and Tony Trigilio.

December

12/28/19

"This in-between condition," Norman writes at the *end* of his poem. So that's where we end this apprenticeship of time? Betwixt. Bewitched by memories that masquerade inside anxiety; a late night awakening to worry over an envelope. First objects blur, and then the persons you knew as clear cut silhouettes in your dorm room or grad school studio. Bits of conversation braid and then fray, winding like damaged DNA in some wacky helix like wisteria on a frame in Japan where the beer is cold as a nearby stream. You try to stop the stream of consciousness but all you get is the syncopation of rain on tin or brown wood, murmur of Chinese characters on a sidewalk, writ in water by old men. Water is another kind of sound, the viola's evaporation in the living room with its plywood floors a marker of days that have fallen off the calendar, as if it were the flat earth and an army prevented us from getting close to the edge. I can't see the day fall, but I know it's happening from my safe room in the rain forest, where there's storage space for memories only, and they keep spilling like hot potato water on my student's foot, a painful red in her Birkenstocks. Birkenstocks are for white people, my daughter surmises, but she finds them fascinating nonetheless. I'm reading about a typist who's lost her voice, and then lost the other voice box that dings at the end of each line, and then her agency (not Temp). The art of losing in this scheme of things involves a broken seam between object and feeling. Objects drop their feelings, even for those who first assigned them. Don't pick up that handkerchief, or you might salvage salt from someone's tears, without remembering when or why they wept. The night Baghdad was bombed. The night Trump was "elected." Those are not objects, but they leave traces. He took a picture of a large round rock, laced with deep lines and green splotches. It seemed a talisman of something. Like the blazing of a trail you cannot find later on. To dissolve a bad memory (so-called), apply alcohol to the relevant synapses, the ones that over-fire at your favorite time of night. Aviations work well. They haven't found the seventh body from a tour helicopter that crashed on Kauai, but they assume another death. To assume is to appropriate. I assume the authority to erase your memories of such trauma as kept you up at night, the years of abuse you cannot begin to abstract; abstraction, like denial, is a form of semi-healing. Do not re-tell the story of a genocide unless you find yourself once again inside of it, as in a barrel full of nails falling off a cliff. The question is how to avoid as many of these nails as possible, pulling them out of either the barrel or your torso, dealing with the collateral damage to both. When this happens in the classroom, you are often unaware until later that your mention of suicide, say, hurt the student whose father threatens it, or the student who attempted it, or the atmosphere of it as a dangling participle in a sentence that's bound to end badly. I used to over-use the phrase "as if," as engine to imagine, but now the "if only" strikes a stronger chord. The ways of the Bodhisattva include gratitude for those who wound you. Family becomes the trope for laceration; to resume that conversation after so many years risks a drawer full of knives, applied randomly to the surfaces of your body. Almost an erotic exercise. It's not the one person who wounds, but the others who witness the attack and detach its object from its subject (you, their friend!). It's the magical contagion of ambition, award system for emotions to be transmuted later into publishing contracts or jobs with a mirage-hope of tenure, for which we sacrifice everything. I left the homeless kits in their freezer bags in the car, smelling of Dove soap.

12/30/2019

In the palace of forgetting an old orator walks toward the scene of a bloody hate crime, to see it evaporate into marble. Dissipation into permanence: only memory loss qualifies. The woman down the street retired as a government wildlife biologist during Bush 2; her mother has dementia, lives in northern Virginia. Chit chat aggregates. Did I finally find a slot for a proper nominalization? To nominalize is to normalize; to normalize is the new ostranenie. It's an avant-garde of realists, bending to take photos of tree ferns, so small you mistake them for mosses. The closer you get to the image, the less it travels away from you, buying a bus ticket to the downhill town, route bending and swerving like a prism-prison. Light ascends and descends on the strand of a web that sways, stock market graph in real time, without the stocks or the market. A sprig of red ginger shines through the green leaf like a silhouette of thorns. Metaphors begin things, but seldom conclude them. Allegory hardly fares better: the movie about a bus in Japan starts in the middle and ends there; lacking plot, we still see a near accident, minor sexual harassment, geometries of flirtation. The driver is not the central character, though without him there'd be no movement, no turning into the tight corner that precedes another line that bends into another, going the way opposite. The bus maps non-narrative, its starts and stops and cigarette breaks. (Remember how cigarettes used to drive the plots!) Realism has none, only instances that promise one, then fail to deliver. The president condemns hate crimes in words he never uses. So far, this is all meta-talk, skating above the exigencies that detail lays out on a table, either to put together like a puzzle, or to slam with a hammer that divorces noun from verb, sill from syllable. The Americans on the bus made me feel ashamed. I hoped no one else spoke English, but of course they did. That was before Trump. When ugliness was still clenched in its bulb, aching to get out in the air to spread its filthy petals. It's all performance, the bud erupting into color, the president exhorting his followers that the opposition "hates" them. (He otherwise talks way too much about love.) We call the one beauty and the other filth, though it's a problem when they appear to coincide. The lovely fascist sprig in a vase by the door. Nothing clears the mind like climate change, Joe writes, unless it's happiness, as the article suggests. "Is that what it's called?" another responds. Can happiness be a form of cynicism? Or is Nandini right when she says what we need is hope and cynicism together? In what order, I should have asked, do we apply this tonic? It's hard to hold them together, like a political form of pathos, this building up in an era of destructiveness. Freedom of religion means we can keep you out, and freedom of press means their freedom to praise and praise only. If the novels disappear, we're left with more bad plotlets, silences laid out like cutlery before we know which tool goes in which hand. After his stroke, he could not easily find his words. "Why did they invite HIM to speak?" But it wasn't the speaking that was powerful, it was the not. There are wooden petal-pegs where the knots were in plywood on the floor. It's not decorative plywood, Bryant says, it's practical. Sometimes to mend is better

than to make. Let's institute a prize for good mainte-
nance.

12/31/2019

The woman in the book shop talks to her little girls in Hawaiian. When they leave, the shopkeeper tells her "the language is so beautiful." You can find Hawaiian dresses for American dolls down the road, the plump white girls in lei and mu`umu`u who stand staring out at Kilauea Avenue. The tea room is in back, says another sign, its arrow pointing toward the street. Three years ago I saw racist graffiti nearby, took photos as a form of erasure. To preserve is to demolish the power of words, maybe. A verb might be a noun that blusters, or noun might be verb with a severe back-ache. The leaves of the invasive ginger slick with rain water, apapane chitter in the canopy. At 60, our ghosts come to keep us company. They don't take up space, but circulate around us. I was always walking behind Marthe; as she was tall, I watched her well-toned calves take on another steep ascent. My dad's scarred index finger ripped mostly off in an old washboard. My mother's narrow chin. Those who are dead we imagine are anxious for their living, offering us warm coats and tea. A deep dishonest decade ends, but tomorrow promises no respite. It's all golf and graft as far as our eyes can see. The woman who was talking to her daughters was asking them to come to her; they ran the narrow alleys between bookshelves, just far enough away to provoke her voice. "I can't even listen to his voice!" my mother said of the first Bush, when he was the only one. Her sister's grandmother lapses into silence, sleeps a lot. Does she still do her word puzzles, I ask. "She just puts a line through the page," her sister says.

January

1/2/2020

An attempt to circumnavigate the present, its minor and major corruptions, as if not to name them were to pull down the blinds, buffer ourselves against its violence. Ghosts walk across my inner eyelids, "paying" visits as one "pays" attention, always the financial metaphor to keep us apart. He got rid of his iPhone because he had completely lost confidence. We wonder what the link is between self-doubt and smart phones, even if we share the hunch. I try to sit with the birds and with the violence, without ignoring either one, as if balance could be achieved from the alternating current of attention. I will not watch the video of an orangutan trying to beat back a bulldozer, but I cannot avoid this morning's photograph of a kangaroo in silhouette against a wall of flame. People have fled in their cars to the beach, another sign the liminal is not benevolent enough. Caught between water and fire, the earth is a narrow band of sand and rock. The prime minister refuses to call a state of emergency while a constituent calls him a "fuck wad" to his face. The crime is in looking, but not seeing; one can see without looking, from behind the blinds where the censor cannot shield you from the 500 million animals dead in Australia, including one third of the population of koala. Like Steve, I'm trying to write a page every day, and like him I wonder what the writing life would be without a censor. He writes that he doesn't know, but I ask if he doesn't at least have a sense of it? Would we be so disdained for our fantasies of pleasure removed from the world's pain? Would we attack ourselves with the fires, in bald imitation of medieval saints, their backs slick with blood from their whips, their minds going into an eclipse from which the soul can't flee? I'm beginning to like these words again, like "soul," precisely for their used up symbolism, their gesture toward feeling, a sense of self as abstraction lodged in an old house. The windows are covered with webs, and with a morning's condensation. When the skies are clear during the day, it gets cold at night. In the morning we rush into our clothes faster than any censor could get us there. Bird song clarity in cold air. One bird sounded like a pig; Bryant thought it a pheasant. Its notes were more round than the apapane's, which chitter from the canopy. To face your pain is not to celebrate it. To put it down is not to relieve it. The elegies for my ghosts will not be salve. Werner Herzog is sure his writing will exist far longer than his films; it's not a matter of quality but of the material on which the art is made. Words are not as fragile as images, and the monkeys taking over an Amazon ship no less memorable as sounds than as pictures. He put a gun to the head of his star, someone told me, to force him to complete the film. Deaths of despair are rising precipitously. The conflagration is our horror film without a script or star. We cannot rewind the narrative, so let's put it out.

The war to prevent war has re-begun. It's hard to be a
saintly nation, certain of its virtues, its kindness, the
generosity of its violence. They are bad men because
they kill us, but we are good men because we remove
them from this earth, by bomb or by drone. It's done.
No matter if we call the play from the office that lacks
corners (he was astonished!) or from the golf course. Its
faux slice of nature does include traps, though they're
easily evaded with a mulligan or two. Just like the con-
voy of death, several wars ago; beside the trucks you
might find family photos or IDs, but inside there was
only ash. Ash falls on the eastern shores of Australia.
He walked through Sydney and "smelt of smoke." I was
surprised by the "smelt," though that is what men do to
metal to make it. When it's hot, it bends, but earth is
more like a paper straw that's been bent so many times
it's wilted, like flowers, like travelers in the heat. But
back to the actual war, not the one we poured gasoline
on before hiding out on a bleached reef or simmering
roof; we're left in an attending position. I waited for
signs of life on the screen, but the tech refused to tell
me what it meant. The phone calls came later. Like se-
cret messages from your enemy, wishing you the worst
as you try to balance hope and cynicism, finally bind-
ing them with ribbon, then putting on a prefabricated
bow for good measure. The festive time of year comes
crashing to a halt with the news cycle, which is one. No
more are linear histories possible; it's all circulation,
traffic circles without exit, an Irish refrigeration truck
bearing down on you from what only seems the wrong

side of the road. When you get to the turn, you have to calculate desire against circumstance, habit against this new frontier of obeying the local laws, shifting with your left hand, steering on the right. Tasman forests burn, the outskirts of Sydney burn, a woman collapses in Canberra from the smoke. Earth dies by our suicide. The writing that's intended to go abstract, intended to avoid the knife in the back that stays in the back, the never healing from this damage, the PTSD that is no laughing matter, the bending over weeping in the kitchen not knowing how a man could do that to a boy, or a nation, or a koala. State flags fly upside down from legions of pick-up trucks. Pam has lost her fight, she writes, but wants to kill every politician in Australia. Grieving her partner's daughter's father and the bush, which is expansive but hardly abstract. The reason Australian irony is so strong, Tranter said, is that if you're in trouble and you leave the city for the bush, you're dead.

1/4/2020

The son bores a hole in his father's skull, releasing his spirit as the body burns. Once charred, it's immersed in the river. Not to put it out but to send it on as product. Her poems were never as good after the one about bathing in the Ganges, feeling ashes and bones jostle around her. Because her mother demanded it. The flip side of spirit is ash. We're doing our very best to create more of it, says no one at Raytheon, though they love their stock prices about now. If we see them as stock figures, they're easier to take out with our drones. Put faculty in small rooms for 12 hours at a time to write free textbooks. Put middle Americans in small rooms for 12 hours at a time to kill a man in Baghdad. Put us all in examination rooms to take our obedience tests. And in lines for phones to prepare us for more deadly ones, but earn no empathy from the experience. Because the state demands it. The woman who dances at half-time still believes in perfection, though she knows it doesn't exist. What does the drone-driver feel when her flying object hits its target? Is there a sense of a job well done, something created of her skill and training? Might she be a good reader of literature, one who finds the precise point the plot shifts and marks it with her pen? I missed the point of Henry James, hurrying to find it after the student with the southern accent performed it in our lounge. Association is a kind of stereotyping, as this next sentence wants to be about Mitch McConnell, slow talking his defense of the despot over whom a flock prays. He began his speech to the faithful by boasting he'd killed a man. They lean over to touch his jacket, bless him because he's a vehicle of the Lord brought to save those unborn babies who are needed to fight our wars. It's not the belief system they've attacked, but our capacity to feel productive doubt. Because, as she claimed, it was all in my imagination, I had a hard time solving the equation that generated anything beyond doubt as IED. We talked in class about what IED means, finally settling on "improvised" as the first word in the acronym. Acrid aid to memory. That was a decade ago, and now we say it again. Not to be found on the stock exchange of Iran, but stenciled on the streets of Baghdad, malign graph to our narrative, confusing climax with denouement, and always death for meaningful life. No arc this, but a more chaotic geometry that cannot be solved for any x. We know the needle on suicide points higher, but that's no sign of order, just of good accounting. The study of gun deaths was banned. Those closing bells do toll for thee and me. So get out your silencers and work on your noise suppression techniques. The loaded gun has gone mute. A river of our blood contains no sacred ash; we've cut out the middle man. Save 20% on plots, a large sign reads at our local cemetery. It blew over in the last storm.

1/6/2020

Abstraction seemed one way to fly over, leaving pesky
details to bloody themselves on prairie or white sand,
but news that the shoreline has receded half a foot a
year since the 1920s puts the fear of god into our met-
aphorical field. She writes that thinking of feelings as
passing clouds does nothing to alleviate her anger over
climate change. A new metaphor would confess to the
current turmoil, highway lined with dead animals in
Australia, war clouds (which are at least dark) gather-
ing over mourners who vow to trade tooth for tooth.
(The metaphor started here, the correspondent says
petulantly.) Who's to argue with prophets or profits?
One prophet got a good sneaker deal and jogs around
the desert with tablet in hand (you can see the Apple
icon in the corner); another drives a Ford truck like the
one vandalized next door. When they meet in commit-
tee to discuss their investment in futures, they weigh
prophecy against loss, aiming to say only enough that
we fill the churches. Our Lady of the Freeways packs
them in! Book deals are crucial, like the one Moses
should have had on his commandments, so don't say
anything out loud until you get your advance. Advanc-
es are what it's all about. Not the avant, whether mili-
tary or art, but cold cash offered before your foretelling
crashes like the Dow. You'd think that with this prog-
nosis the name of the game would be self-help: How to
Abide the Coming Crisis. But the gang of eight or ten
or twenty-four knows other books sell better: How to
Construct Your Anti-Nuclear Hut, or How to Write
Love Letters to Dear Leader. In that instance, you need

only spell out your sycophancy, knowing it a difficult spell. (Took me three tries, with spell check.) Exaggerate your words of affection, and never tease the Leader, because he lacks social skills. Just pinch pen and make your strokes broad and straight and bold. Do not hold back; mixed feelings are no longer permitted by writ of the packed court. Do not entertain any judge who hesitates to mete out punishment, or any leader who fails to threaten destruction of cultural sites. "War crimes" were already a contradiction in terms, so why obey a hollow rule? Remember when we failed to bomb them into the stone age? Second chances happen for those who wait. It's the quarterback's fault we're a divided people. All that kneeling and no tackling. No wonder he hasn't had a job since. But I've dropped my too too happy abstraction, strained my tea for too long in the brown waters of the river, call it Babylon. A neighbor up the hill's license plate reads TIGRIS. From One to Another Paradise, the tour brochure might read. We take you from the base of sheer tropical mountains to the river where civilization began. You return home to smoke your weed on Sundays. We've broken chronology, pulled it all into the present tense, heard you calling in air strikes in Ahuimanu. At the Mauna, Spring promises bulldozers and men in electric green shirts. Until then, attend to the birds and trucks.

If you put boulders on sand, gravel on boulders, the coastal road on gravel, the road will eventually collapse, not because ocean pushes boulders, but because sand's an unstable foundation. Gravity does the rest. If you build a tunnel through the mountain, expect landslides and fallen trees. If you build desert townhouses in a rain forest, expect the walls to be damp, the ceilings to peel away. "It's always been like that and always will be," says the white man with the one-eyed dog, as my dog sniffs his. His voice dissonant: "those rag heads hate us because we are." Another neighbor suggests asking for precision: does he mean Indians or Sikhs? Does he mean the people we just attacked? Does he use a towel when he dries his head after a shower? Specificity's important when you're from the South, he says. I'm reminded a high school teacher loved the Plath line, "the horses are," which ended with the verb for *being* without movement, drama of existence not action. My cat sits beside me, considers leaping up on the bed, leaps; outside rooster call and mower construct an awkward chord. In Volcano, a philosophy prof's organizing a conference on anarchy at the military camp. It all depends on how you parse the verb or noun, because sometimes they mean twice. Jon notes that "mean" also means "mean." Anarchy as chaos or as alternate order. It must be exhausting to be so angry, I want to say to my neighbor down the street. What father or what war made you so angry? Was it a boy scout leader who groomed you away from the crowd, had his way with you for years, while shame crashed down like a curtain before a bombing raid? And why did you put a fluffy white collar around the tiny dog you walk each day, faithfully? He was a bad man, but so are you. My twitter feed warns me that photographs of dead animals in Australia are graphic, and the warning alone triggers something in me, like avoidance, or the desire to write. I write because it grounds me, a colleague says, when everything else is chaos. It's that search for meaning, road on gravel on boulder, and gravity takes it down as soon as the typing ends. Some form of entertainment, this meaning. Absorptive as a video game, and just as interactive, but the hours away from the monitor are blank, at best. I meditated to the sound of a video game and a tv show; our attention is there to be grabbed. Sexual predators come to court in wheelchairs or with walkers. One reached out for the railing as an aide pulled his walker away; he stuttered up the stairs. The dharma talk was on judgment, how corrosive it is. Negative thinking takes up much of our time, a study determined. I could ask the man with the one-eyed dog to think happier thoughts. "It's all in your imagination," I would say; "you think too much." But the orthodontics of emotion take more time than that. I signaled my virtue, turning on my heel, telling him he was a racist. Short cut; stale, mate.

1/9/2020

Choose a color, any color, and meditate on that. Find 100 meanings of your color and write two pages on each, making sure to consider figurative, as well as literal, meanings for red or green or blue or white. Why does no one count the "hapa" vote, a friend asks, when everyone else has their block? The Filipino musicologist defined "local" by moving us from Oahu to the Philippines to a province to a city to a street to a block to an apartment. Doubtless there are localities in the liver, since you can give away a part to be grown later. There's discipline in detail, like the military chants my father made as we marched down apartment corridors; it was good father-daughter fun then. Consider the different valences of white: orchid, dove, voting block, men with tiki torches marching in the street. Days after posting a video opposed to racism against Muslims, my son put a blue line American flag on his car. So long as you employ it, the symbol is no longer yours. It's a hive to which a colony returns, adamant in their stinging praise of the leader, for once a woman. The drones dare not differ, nor even higher-ups, forced as they are to recant, spill honey from their lips, appease the tyrant queen. The hive is on his head beneath the orange pompadour. My mother remembered Elvis in Friedberg in the 1950s, driving a truck. Men in Tokyo congregate of a Saturday to participate in his mirror stage, strutting through the park walk like dark roosters. I heard a pellet gun, saw a rooster across the parking lot jerk and then fall; a neighbor walked calmly over, put rooster in trash bag, headed to the dumpster. The roosters sit in a tree behind their house and sing all night long. Elvis was Memphis Jesus, before and after King died for our sins. No surface in that man's house (West Point, Virginia, circa 1975) was without its black velvet or its statuette. When asked what the President has done that he likes, a young man in red hat stutters, stops. He has taken our breath away with his gyrating tongue, his pacing up and down the stage, his one liners about how much They hate Us, his sexy calls for violence. It's not funny, but they laugh, and that gives them license. A man dropped his license in front of me at the Mall yesterday, and then I walked outside, where a woman pushing a baby in stroller dropped her coat. I kept pointing at what was getting lost, walking to my car after ordering new lenses that won't make me so dizzy. Introduce your neighbor using only the information you find on their driver's license. Symbolic value is as corruptible as any. Launder your flags with your greenbacks. *Try use bleach.*

1/10/20

It's a story they tell themselves that makes sense of their lives, he says. A story links race to rape, rape to the military, hence to America's wars of imperialism and back to rapes, to orphans. Then throw adoption in. Take the walkers away from sex offenders, someone writes, so they can't provoke our pity. They can walk after they're declared not guilty, can't they? He had a good experience in the Boy Scouts, but his abuser had been a scout leader. He had an abuser who was a scout, but his grandfather was a kind man. Variables sing out from flawed equations, demanding restitution. There's need for a Rage Park where we can pause to scream, throw bones to ourselves and chase them, unleash ourselves in a controlled space. The problem with containing rage is that it resists the container, spills through netting or chain link that holds it in. An arm across the chest signals love and confinement. The wedding photo showed his arm around her neck. The murder dressed as suicides came later. Someone left the abuser to die in his cell and threw out the video evidence. It means denial can masquerade as hope. It's not just trauma we push down, mistaking silence for safety. It's also positive emotions that go into hiding in the city's sewers or basements, those things with feathers avoiding the street, angling for cultural amnesia. A schoolyard fills with terrified kangaroos, fleeing the bush fires. Bet you hadn't expected that migration. Texas will take no more refugees, as they've done their share. Who parcels out these shares, or keeps the graphs of their rise and fall? Who has victimized whom? Do not look at yourself in the mirror. I posted the photograph of a dead saffron finch on instagram; it lay belly up on the sidewalk beside the culvert, its neck so bright a yellow it appeared orange, with fragile orange beak. Does the photograph preserve or desecrate the bird? It garners lots of likes. Is it the beauty of the dead bird's plumage, or the framing of bright color by gray sidewalk? Decomposition composed. Camera as stun gun, fired at whatever you least want to change. Or can least resuscitate. My daughter finds it odd that I take pictures of dead birds; she saw a dead mouse, but refused. The Tibetan monks who meditate beside a charnel pit are not so shy. To see oneself as flesh, then bone, then dust, makes our being's imminent absence visible. Immanence is no lie, though the stories the President tells are yarns. A friend took photos of homeless persons' blankets, so as not to invade their privacy. She holds up the brightly colored quilt she made for her son. The last ever, she swears. Make sure your conclusion is less an ending than an opening, and leave off the moral of every story told.

I am just a peg to hang his cursive meditations on. When I ask my students to offer up a quirk, one says he's an English major who doesn't read. He used to read half a book before he put it down, but now he doesn't get that far. Very few in our generation read much, says my daughter's friend, the one who's reading Thich Nat Hanh on dying. At night they turn on *Baywatch* for the bodies, not the plot. But bodies *are* the plot, machines to make prompts for our writing exercises, the ones our parents worry about because we can't make money off them. She realized quickly that thinking might help her earn money, so she went to class. I argue for inherent value, but that's as quaint as poetry. Do nothing for ten minutes a day, I put on my syllabi; if this seems too hard to fit in, remember it's a course requirement. If I could give credit, I would, but the value inheres in practice and practice makes good enough. Somewhere in the middle of that question, statement took over, the rhetorical hammered into bronze, like a statue that walked out to sea at the end of a novel I've forgotten. If earning is like memory, accruing value over time, then forgetting takes us back to living within our meaning. A small bird sits outside my window on the brown rhapis palm frond, but when I look back from my writing, it's gone. We await the dropping of the next shoe. It's hard to fight corruption, because it's spongy, and it gives and gives before folding into itself, feeding the next salted wave of paranoia. It's formalism, really, but without irony; the more you work at the poem's structure, the less you find between the ribs. I explain my dog's name by citing the woman who didn't require a man's rib. Hard power defeats soft every time, with occasional exceptions for martyred saints. Her personality is extremely rare, as she puts connections over division, others above herself. Another student comes from a family of six kids and two parents, all of them vegan. Sitting beside her is the woman who likes the all-you-can-eat meat bar. It's a diverse society, but you have to be taught to express yourself. He governed his tongue in class because the toxic TA policed everyone's words. We want everyone to be better, so we demand specific sentences of them. A man on the radio said (this was in the late 60s) he thought "brainwashing" was when you took someone's brain out of their body and gave it a bath. For our next class, consider why we write while Australia burns.

1/16/20

The actor who plays Glenn Gould drives an old car (it was newer then) and nods his head to Judy Collins' "Downtown." She's still singing in the truck stop (always the same thing on the radio back then, I advise my students). He wears dark glasses, the better to retreat behind his ears. One student said her sense of smell is hyperactive because she doesn't hear well. The conversations form a fugue, so I play them one, though they can't hear Gould's droning voice from where they sit. The room is way too cold. Another student says his name lacks the second "r" found in Trump's son's name. He's adamant on that fact. Note that voices are also "voices" in the music, that his finger wants to play keys, but only reaches his coat, that "it's over!" occurs in English, while the interlocutor's slow-voweled French sounds unintelligibly sad. "It's about eavesdropping," one student exclaims. It's the poetics of my pedagogy, I think, these few minutes of attending to others' sounds and organizing them into music. "Then I'll do my majic," writes the Ukrainian thug, or was it his boss? The thug has a comical comb-over, his very few strands of greasy hair pushed forward to meet the cowlick that grazes on his forehead. One student wrote in his exquisite corpse that it was getting harder to fold the pieces of paper. A materialist of the word! We write to express ourselves, while he speaks to accuse the other of acting in as malign a fashion as he does. With projection comes the possibility of a tear in the film, one you have to salvage for now with scotch tape, unless you let the reel run itself apart from any images on the screen. A coyote running off a cliff gets some time to think about hanging in the air, the fall he's about to take, the inevitable starting over (since he *is* a cartoon). If only we could rewind the deaths of despair. I went to clean up after a Fellini film, but the last reel was Jerry Lewis, and everyone was filing out of the auditorium confused. Is "inherent value" simply another phrase for "art for art's sake," hence a wee bit decadent? Or is it the lung that blows into a balloon that looks down on battlefield or tulip field for once able to breathe because detached from the earth? One student wants to escape reality in her next life by becoming a unicorn. They're pretty, she says. The exquisite corpse, he notes, doesn't tell a story. In what world is the unicorn real? Or is there space outside the real, even for the fictional character in her own world, which we might otherwise *call* real, lacking a bigger lexicon? She took "I am not a crook" for "cook," but that was the fault of my bad handwriting.

1/18/2020

The right wing commentator opines, we must forget what the enablers said 20 years ago; it's their job to defend the president, not to tell the truth. Formalism is one tool of the fascist state, narcissism another, the formalism of the Self as a real entity, not the lousy abstraction theologians make of it. Parents cringe at poetry seminars, I read in the paper, which do nothing to make their children marketable. My students note a similarity between poetry and advertising, but it costs less to jump straight into the pun as a lever of desire, rather than an expression of it. What does it mean, that the GDP of Bhutan is happiness? That it's a poor country, I wager. The smile is symbolic, and everyone knows symbols govern poems and poems govern nothing (or make it happen). Better to learn the art of serving the rich, who have transcended art. As Steve notes, this is not a diary, nor can it be parsed for any metrical value. We make art on the rebound, but we haven't yet hit bottom. Will you write more books, my friend asks, saying she has but one more book in mind. She's not afraid to die, she says, as the phone connection unravels. The tapestries of friendship are what remain; we say the word "love" to one another more than ever before to ease the pain of bullying. Why climb the rungs, when each frames another act of cruelty? I cannot begin to imagine the stations of hell in Dante's university: the dictates of purity demand that you speak only with delicacy inside your own office. Do not tell a student what might be reported as critique, even if that word has other currency. Or you might find yourself walking toward averted eyes, or freshly turned backs. She wants to kill me, one says, meaning not in the literal sense, but in one every bit as painful. The artist is she who believes her metaphors are true. It's not that they want another truth, because truth is beside the point. They want a weaponized sentence system that will take out the anti-aircraft of evidence-based arguments, burn the tender feeling in the latest psalm read in church. Do not condemn anyone for their bad acts, because you are capable of the same. Instead, attend to your own nave and altar. Then pun on them to expand your range! My new glasses distort less, correct the astigmatism in my left eye. Your eyes are very different, the doctor said, that's why it's so hard to correct them. If you need glasses, you don't work through the bad habits that damaged your vision. But who needs correction if there's a buzzer on your chest to signal fastball or change-up, curveball or slider? Astrophil and Stella must have their title stripped. The sonnet's all fake news, there's no market for its rhymes or limp sentiments.

The world ends in hail and dust. No more a consistent tense that moves from present to present, but a tense confabulation. It's a powerful move, I tell my students, but you need to know where you're going. It's not that we're all living in the present, rather that its fragile shell so easily shatters. Memory loses all category, as if the past only rewound the present. My mother confused my story with hers, my husband with hers. Who's to say we were not all on that plain, huge orange dust storms sweeping toward us, enveloping our drone-witness, bearing material prophecy in its grit? The dust cloud is 186 miles long and moves at 66 miles per hour; it crests over Dubbo and Broken Hill, composed of earth from farms in New South Wales. "Look at the earth," my father would say, meaning the orange clay that only broke when you took your spade to it. The earth was that color in Vietnam, a vet told me. But now it rises as if it had wings and its poet wasn't always so stoned he heard angels singing, their verbs blooming dutifully at the ends of sentences, where they propel us back to the beginning, no matter their tense. Our witnesses watch for us, a drone hovering over Diamond Head to see how many houses burned on the first clear day in weeks. It was such a beautiful day. Without my uttering the word, my students talk about mindfulness, this being in the present, being with, not coming after. Legions of bearded white men descend on Richmond with their guns; one chides a younger man for using the word "masturbation." We're here to show our love for each other, he says, and the younger man avers, backing off. One wears a knitted American flag hat, the other an orange bandanna. Love does not alter where it alteration finds, is bronzed like another horseman in another instagram photo. Yesterday, I saw Ronald Reagan on a horse, as still as a church mouse. The drone came back to the park like a boomerang, though after the third news story it's running in the present, coming back and back to spill its video record. She read out loud from *To the Finland Station*, sentences unspooling like Krapp's tapes, students giggling at their heft. At the Atocha Station, I thought I saw old women selling bats on sticks, suspicious that the poem was an act of realism, not experiment. There was a plaque for the intervening dead. Some species may be rendered extinct by the bush-fires. To be going extinct. What tense is that? The continuous perishing.

She says the neighbor was sitting on his truck bed while his daughter played on the swings yesterday. Today, he told me he was close to both of the dead officers. Marcus Aurelius writes that we observe everything before we're 40. From then on, it's a loop. We get used to things; we put a distance between us and our injuries; we reconcile ourselves. We forgive the trespasses of those who trespass against us. (Wisdom literature leans forward and back.) Aurelius would recognize the absurdity of this weekend's violence: an old man killed cops with a shotgun, then set his neighborhood on fire. If reality presses against our eyelids, then how can we close our eyes? We keep them open to our devices, real and imagined. Distraction may have gotten us here, but it had better save us now. An Englishman once asked me why Americans use "gotten" instead of "got" as a verb form. I assured him we do not. Two sentences later, I heard myself say "gotten." How little we know ourselves by our verb forms. They make a fine family tree, however, enough to launch a holy book. Had he gotten help, he might not have run amok, the angry Czech. I want a how-to on looking, while not suffering for it. If I make my sentences longer, they might lose their hurt before the period waves its penalty flag. Can I offer wisdom before the facts, like a trial set up to occur before any witnesses are called? It's a rough path, life, my son writes, though his photograph is of a wall. No matter the angle, the edges are blunt and sharp, and each fork in the road gets you there. The president has done nothing wrong, his counsel says, so there's no need to introduce evidence. We're watching the death of democracy on our screens, but it's not entertaining enough, so we'll do it quickly. No wonder our tenses are inconsistent. What occurred before the trial must be presented after the trial is done. Acquit him first, then argue that the evidence comes in too late. There's a crisis in comedy, but I haven't watched any for years now. The transcript of an absurdity is like a garden tool used to injure your landlord. "Kill da landlord," Eddie Murphy screamed. It was funny then, but it isn't the day after the landlord cannot be found dead in her own home, burned to the ground by her tenant. You can't tell the joke, if the punch-line comes first. Or the shotgun blast. She let him stay in the house because she pitied him.

1/24/2020

The man with the blank map keeps calling you into his office. The man with the blank map in his office points to blank portraits on the wall. We see that they were men, but they are featureless. All that's left of their histories shows in gilded frames, cleansed of dirt, that glint beneath the ceiling lights. The blank map man screams profanities, but the next day he will attack you for your "lack of decency." The blank faced men in frames cannot look out or in. A senator refers to himself as "visibly upset"; perhaps he has a selfie to prove it, because neither in nor out will do what at requires. Look within thyself and write, or look at thyself and whine. A good portrait keeps his eyes on you as you cross the room. The eye that sees you is more powerful than a weapon, because it gives you pause to think. "People will hear about this," said the man with the map, intending it as a threat. What is most dangerous is someone else's attention to us. I will sit quietly in my office. I will not say to anyone what they might repeat to another. My mask is a map with nothing on it. I know it covers a place, but I cannot stick a pin in that place. The memory police are out to shame us, but shame has no currency. None of my students ever drew the face of a quarter with any accuracy. We cannot see what we use. A gumball means more than a founding father. Chew on that.

I hadn't seen him in a while, the gray-haired white man who walks the one-eyed dog named Rosie, sometimes yells at traffic to stop. He'd yelled at me, too, about Hillary, about lazy millennials, about the university, about how people just don't look out for each other any more, about people who drive through stop signs. A radical centrist, he called himself. For months after, I talked about his dog and mine, the weather, anything neutral (weather over climate, I'm sure). The last time we'd met, just past the new year, he'd yelled at me about "rag heads," and I called him a racist. Turned on my heel. Today, as I came up Hui Kelu with Lilith, I saw him and Rosie ahead of us. He saw us. At his turn-around point, he crossed the road, started back toward his townhouse on the next street over. He had sunglasses on, wrap-arounds. I said, "good morning!" but he kept going. His body clenched tight: arms out from his sides, legs moving like pegs. The only softness to him might be his belly. He's my lesson, but it's a lesson I cannot learn. Perhaps he's happy in his horrible opinions, a friend opines, but I don't believe it. He's how pain turns to Fascism; he's how hurt accumulates grudges; he's how you come to hate a woman neighbor who wears an Obama shirt, so clearly a "snowflake," even in paradise. He's how you don't avoid your pain, but alchemize it into anger. It's more valuable that way. He's how you take someone aside, abuse her, and then call her indecent. He's how the mirror works. The man who yells at traffic sees me on his mirror, but not as myself. This confuses me, like the times my demented mother

44

transposed herself on me. So accustomed to seeing myself in the mirror, I saw the image of someone I didn't want to be.

1/30/2020

On the Friday the Republic dies, there will be a sale on our words. They're more valuable to us as empty containers than as pith. The store that sells us on organizing will stack them at the windows, inviting us to use "democracy" to store our beans, "due process" to hold our rough drafts. My students find the sonnets uninteresting, incomprehensible. Yes, there's a speaker in the poems, and yes, he's hectoring a friend. He wants his friend to "breed." He wants his friend to last forever, as a collection of words. But we'll sell those, too, like the banana taped to a wall that sold for $250,000 before someone walked up and ate it. The banana gives us mental energy; I may be remembering my former students' names because I ate one this morning. It's useful, and to suggest otherwise is a joke. An expensive one. They shake their heads at the thought. Is it a joke on intrinsic value, on art's rot, on the usefulness of duct tape, or do we take it at its word: "banana"? I'd tape mine to a wall if I could, then take your good money to dispatch it. If I no longer own the word "idealism," I cannot be disappointed when it proves useful in a service economy. The word "hoard" explains a lot; so does the border wall that falls in a stiff wind. One field has to do with economies of love, the other its sickness. The best words aren't just empty; they're translucent in the way plastic is, admitting light while blocking clarity. The former dive instructor said there were days she surfaced into fields of plastic. I urged her to start there; that's an image we can hold onto. Beneath the ground-cover this morning, I saw a yellow toy smile at me. I took its picture.

February

2/2/20

She knew a woman who lived in the house of the woman who died at the hand of her tenant, by fire or by gunshot. The woman who owned the house worked in the library; she looked familiar. She belly-danced. I might have seen her at the old Egyptian place, a middle-aged white woman thrusting her belly forward, my friend's partner's straying eye but brief. Anne was guardian ad litem at a house where a sumo wrestler was killed over meth. Next door, a young mother beat her son when his kind step-dad was away. Up the hill, a man keeps his disabled parents hostage on the lower floor, while he goes surfing in his van. We tell ourselves it's always been bad. That despair is their friend, not ours. The practice is about facing death, but we think of that death as ours, not our republic's by which it stands, one nation indivisible, with. The poems aren't so much about love but the damage we leave, if we're lucky. He wants to translate old poems into new, render them honest in their confessions to inadequate feeling. I open the old poet's book and find an inscription—to me,—"with love," two days after a birthday. He gave me a bear hug in a thick sweater. Lived in an old fire house with his poet's wife and children. Paid ambivalent homage to Stevens, though he was a Williams man. This is what it will be like, Bryant says, putting one foot in front of the other, not calling attention to yourself, not saying what might be reported. Cloak your words, as in a poem. (And take his name out next time.) The reader comes later, but there will be no trace of you at your place of work. Soon to be acquitted, the president rescinds the ban on landmines. Just because he's guilty doesn't mean we should evict him.

A friend posts a photograph of her table at a cafe. It's not a trendy place, more a greasy spoon. She sits in the shadows, looking out at a couple who've found a window; though we see nothing through it, there is a streak of light at photo's end. The image belongs on a feed of "uninteresting photographs." This is where she sat, she writes, when democracy died. When I go back to look again, I can't find the photo. Like a lapsed memory, it twitches behind my frontal lobe, analogue to a culture's self-lobotomy. "I'm sorry for your loss," a Canadian student says. Usually, there's somewhere to put the loss, in cupped hands, or in a box. But your fingers pull apart and sand pours through. The local woman in the short story turned to sand when she grew upset about her island's history. She was like a human sandbox without the frame. The sand doesn't measure time, it scatters it. Inability to remember sequence is a symptom of trauma; the inability to look another in the eye a symptom of narcissism, which works both ways in this equation. Make it simple, he tells his mother, before and after she unloads a wave of unnecessary detail. We cannot lose what we so completely say, or so we think. Yesterday's meditation turned to the two knots on either side of my spine, held in place by a cage of taut muscles. To what do we hold, when our core is weak? I pull the cushion out from under me and put it between my back and the wooden wall. The wall offers some support, letting my knots' pain loosen. The tree of my spine rests against the lumber of the wall, soon to be torn down to make open space. From the next cushion over, I hear my neighbor say she meditates by elimination: first goes the grocery list, then the student papers, then the pesky colleague. Her daughter's moods can be witnessed in the behavior of her cats. She recognizes her new cottage by the pencil sharpener on an outside beam. She's always been obsessed by pencil sharpeners. Wood curls and drops to the ground, beside the much loved cat, imported from another friend's photo-stream.

The question of surfaces came up. We can call content a surface, if it carries a mirror on the other side. We can call the mirror depth, so long as we stack it on others. Ron calls it torque, what happens between sentences, but I'm more inclined to call it cliff, or canyon. Mules no longer traverse Molokai's cliffs, so our friend walked up to buy supplies, then 3600 feet back down. It took a day to go shopping, and detergent was heavy. My student calls it "abyss," but he's young yet. After we read Sonnet 73 and I play the role of the older poet to the younger man, another student asks if I'm dying. To grow older is not to read but re-read, which is to look for something other than content (note the pun). Tell me why the sentence is beautiful, and assign it a role in its paragraph. Does it serve as function or as mini-poem? If you open the mini-poem, are you charged $12 to buy a guaranteed A paper, or do you get to drink from it for inherent value? If we call each other service workers, clients, and consumers, what is left for the rootless, the suffering, the unattached? She turned the noun "snake" into verb, transformed the garden hose into a sentient being. You can make the sentence dull by ejecting metaphors, so we do. There's a hose on the sidewalk. I remember seeing a snake in the grass in Kingston, New York, thinking at first it was a hose, then noting its thickness, the way it moved away from us kids through something that appeared to be volition. We only read character through action, unless we read the sonnets well. The metaphor serves a function, but falls off meaning's cliff-edge. A tiny parachute appears, negotiating the walls between sentences, and you brace yourself against the canyon floor. When you listen to a woman walking down the stairs (she carries a trash bag over one shoulder), what do her steps sound like? Which are louder, which softer? What does that tell us about the space? My percussionist sits at the table counting out the poem's beats. There's meaning there, but it's parasite to the words. Her dog jumped toward the leaves in their descent. Fill in the second half of that analogy, making a sentence of it. We do have limits, but they're stories that spool out. Rain doesn't fragment the earth; it fills it in. And then a thrush's song leans against the gutter's drips. A rooster stands in the field, for once quiet. Someone's alarm bleats a greeting. Let's try this all again.

We walked past the biker bar in Hilo; a white bearded guy in leather huddled with an Asian woman in leather. I stopped to take a photo of the Trump sticker on a bike, American flag in the shape of a menacing helmet placed neatly on a shiny bumper. "The owner of that bike is right here. He's a Marine!" the woman called out to me. "Take his photo!" I turned to look at them, smiling on the sidewalk. "I'm a Warren woman," I said. They went back in the bar, the woman yelling "four more years." Later, as we sat at the Conscious Cafe, they screamed away on their bikes. I noticed she had her own. Pat, who told us about the five hindrances, started to cry after loving kindness meditation. I couldn't know why. The woman who hadn't been there remembered last week's self-consuming sentence about knowing oneself as god, before god fell away, then knowing. She talked about the problem of self-judgment. On a well-worn facebook thread, one woman said we should not judge the dead; only god can do that. And so we purify our grief, spill turpentine on it, pluck up the pesky patches of rust. Complexity would wreck our grief. I found a slip of paper with his name on it. In pencil were directions to the correct train, given me by a woman who spoke English. The young woman in a Yankees dress laughed at our inability to communicate. Sonnet 130 in ASL reminds a student of how his roommate dances. It's translation back to movement from the word, the beat, effect of the affect spilling from his flowering hands. What do we do with the beauty of these images, the stable climate they assume? How might we say her teeth were bleached coral, her cheeks burned in the Antarctic sun? If we know our history, which moment do we live in? The character's itinerary was abrupt. Each time he traveled, he lost his clothes and had to steal more on the other side. He aged; he grew younger. He met his wife as a child, then saw her after he died, the victim of her father's gun (which none but us will never know). His mother sat on the Chicago train, young again. There are advantages to his condition, he says. Correspondances à Paris reminded me of Baudelaire, and Baudelaire reminds me of prose. In the middle of his sonnet, my student said he was writing prose, then failed to decipher my handwriting, when I replaced it with "verse." Association involves images disguised as words, their surfaces burning like plastic in a new toaster oven. The president's limo drove once around the Daytona track. It was illegal, but he called them all patriots. Our new cast iron frying pan came dangling an American flag.

He asked for the word for times he floated near the ceiling while his uncle molested him below. It's what saved you, a survivor responds: internal space travel--though decades later clocks strike back, as your absent self falls to the floor of that tiny room. After eating the pink edible, I wanted to get outside my body, so I walked to the porch where the air was cool. But the body is always there to be returned to, like a husk or house. Dreams are fictive itineraries. The young poet appears ecstatic as he pronounces the name, *James Baldwin*. He writes a sonnet to Baldwin's face, which doesn't reveal coral teeth or rosy cheeks. It's the crevices of his voice I loved, the wandering up of his cigarette smoke. I want to point to how history and memory intersected in his face, the violence that cut it. But I can't find an indirect way to map roads that cross other roads in a seemingly vacant space. Every fork in the road clenches its teeth in Thomas Hardy novels. Serendipity's no longer a private matter. It feels more like conspiracy every day. "I realized I hadn't thought of Trump for a couple hours," he said, surprised. He's internalized himself as shame. When I went for my appointment, I told the ob/gyn that I thought of him as my legs opened to her speculum's advance. Don't worry, he's not here, she said. You survive by thinking otherwise.

2/23/2020

I walked past all the mirrors in the hallway and nothing showed. There were moments when a flower blossomed, but its petals dissolved on the linoleum floor. I thought I saw a nose lead me from the glass, but it, too, evaporated, leaving only a wave of my imperceptible body in the still air. And then it happened again at the elevator, the mailbox, wherever someone had eyes not to see. The invisible man bathed himself in stolen light. Here light is freely given, but eyes take in what they refuse to give out. Up the street, some Filipino men empty out a house; it was where the gap-toothed Hawaiian man showed me his puakenikeni tree, the one ringed by small plastic horses. Last time we crossed paths, he said he hadn't seen us in a while; I noted the path Lilith now took to the graveyard. A hospice worker sometimes parked out front. "The house is a total mess," the Filipino man says to me. The tree that once held a hundred plastic dinosaurs bears fruit. There was a woman in the house but I never saw her. Her wheelchair sat outside the garage, folded up. Now it's in the yard, surrounded by what can be re-used: some chairs, upholstered and not; old wooden furniture; plastic bins, one containing a garden hose; a faded red cooler.

March

3/3/20

The president, we're told, is deeply engaged; he asks about the market all the time. That we believe. Lilith's spiky ball a corona virus; plastic sun wakes into needles of orange light.

Those who don't know history are condemned to re-
peat it, but there's no repetition, only contagion. What
matter if the stock market crashes on truth or rumor, it
crashes. *Contain and contagion* begin as cons. So does
the president, and there he ends, red hat to orange hair,
promising a stop because, after all, none of this ever be-
gan. Don't buy the knife when the knife is falling at you,
Bryant says of the stock market. All the stock tropes are
trotted out for effect, including the woman who nods,
the gray-haired man who stares ahead, and the other
whose hand is on the president's shoulder not as reas-
surance but as restraint. Contagion is circulation, like a
public library whose books go from island to island, but
always return to their home branch. Be sure to maintain
social distancing and wash your hands constantly. An
army of Lady Macbeths takes to the stage to show us
how, and Weird Sisters stir their pots in steamy circles.
We can't see the gobs of blood, but we know they're
there, even if they smell more like strawberry jam from
the lower seats. It's the tone we can't tune, frantic os-
cillations between serious and absurd panic, this being
punked by a germ that resembles my dog's spiky ball.
When she pushes it with her nose, it squeaks. Plastic
laughter to match organic. She used the word to mark
her illness on a grocery list, while others wrote "toilet
paper" ten times on the blackboard, vowing not to buy
the last roll again. The central scene—Stalin's death—is
funny, but digressions are pure horror, which leads me
to wonder how regression fits. We regress from the seri-
ous center in the dull suburbs, except in this case, where

Siberia's suburbs are central to the moral panic. I cast my eye to the side to see the word count jump. When I asked the older man how he was, he turned his eyes to the right, away from mine. His wife needed surgery after a fall in the night, then he'd been carjacked at the end of a shotgun in Hilo. Even I recognized the female perp in the paper; her second carjacking in nearly as many months. His practice kept him calm; he got their license plate number. His new role is to care for his wife, learn to cook and clean. The newspaper refers to him only as "the elderly man" so often it becomes a mantra for his presumed incapacity. One section of the book ends with the word "perfidy"; it has to do with "chance movement," which either gives or takes away. The seeming chance in a sestina enables the poet to begin in this world and then to make it dream. The garden you see outside the house is drawn in by the inscrutable child.

3/18/20

A turtle's tear, as the butterfly drinks it.

The problem is one of scale: word after word accrues a viral load. We toss the metaphor in the dumpster, but that's an unclean box, prone to excess. Teaching on-line encourages other viruses to spread. A worm vomited bits of my poems to all my contacts: one got miscarriage, the other adoption. To talk on-line is to acknowledge abstraction, a pane of glass between a son and his famous father. The difference between a cat's scream inside or outside the house. When the old woman died, she left behind a beautiful parlor, the gift of a Jewish girl she saved. Touch the brocade and carved wood; it disintegrated in maroon and gilded dust. Our losses were pre-conscious until the day all the emails came flooding in. It's a big wave washing through, and it will be gone, the president said a week ago, before he started alluding to deaths and higher poll numbers. The Fed makes him happy. She'd closed her door on everyone to preserve her secret. It was a real door, but in the context of the novel, it was also symbolic. She closed her border to the alien intruder, the neighbor who sought meaning behind shutters and a garden wall. Meaning foreclosed declares bankruptcy, takes the house of our being and pulls it down from within. First comes the dry wall, and then the beams, everything but the shell. The house cries like a turtle, but no butterfly drinks. I've got ashes near the television and others in the closet. I don't know where to scatter them. A scattered brain is more conducive to anxiety than to accountancy. Everyone told her she was creative, but her mistake was not to become an accountant. She loved to count numbers as they went up and down in her checkbooks, the ones that would have been her memoir had we saved them. I'm left with a few lists of what she had for lunch. I want to account for my life and hers, but I can't keep the numbers straight. The only job I was fired from was one entering data in a spread sheet. She was like Crusoe but I live on the island to which you are dis-invited to visit. Do not drink at our bars, eat at our restaurants, fill our hospitals with your tourist asses. The grown girl had no time to visit her savior. The writer had no time to save the savior. The protagonist died on her way from the bed to the door. Remember, the poet advises, that suffering is your door. No angle will save you.

I want to write a coherent meditation, one that poses a problem and then investigates it like a good detective, turning over the neighbor's rocks to find what lives beneath them, whether lizard or insect. But as I compose my meditations, they fall apart, scatter, perform the entropy that is both addition and subtraction. I never concentrate well, especially not during these days leading inexorably toward pandemic. Near the end of *The Door*, by Magda Szabó, however, I find a place to pause, to locate meaning, perhaps because the scene is one of meaning losing itself into dust, of history crumbling into the privacy of one woman's memory.

The "writer" whose servant master lives in the adjoining house, never opening her door to anyone, enters the back room after her servant's death. Its contents have been promised to her. They came from a Jewish family whose little girl the servant sheltered from the Nazis; she shows up in the novel as an adult too busy to see her protector for lunch. But we don't yet know who she was. The room comes to her from the distant past, untouched by history, but not by history's wear and tear. The writer begins to examine the furniture. She's warned by the Lieutenant Colonel not to touch: "The covers have perished," he tells her; "the furniture's dead. Everything here is dead, except the clock." But she doesn't listen, and grasps the drawer of a console. It refuses to open to her touch. "Suddenly, everything around me became a vision out of Kafka, or a horror film: the console collapsed. Not with a brutal swiftness but gently, gradually, it began to disintegrate into a river of golden sawdust." Nothing remained but dust. Woodworm was the ostensible villain, but the symbolism of the baroque and guarded room dissolving into dust is clear.

There's always been rot at the heart of the Republic, but usually there were a few good carpenters or re-upholsterers to keep up appearances. If a beam started to fall, someone built a brace. If the roof leaked, someone patched it. If our grammar fractured, we found an orator to speak through it. But during these days of self-quarantine (we are all Thoreau now, even if we can't afford to be), I have the sense that our institutions are little more than dead furniture. We might be able to pipe some virtual furniture in through our computers (the world's museums are offering their wares for free!), but what we see, we know, is not what exists in front of us. Materiality is some consolation. But now we're given walls of pixels and asked to remake ourselves in their image, even as the president enacts his racist literalism. "It's 'China flu' because it started in China," he tells us. An Indian American woman standing behind him swallows hard.

The Lieutenant Colonel asks the writer if she wants the clock, which is still running, even though the room has evaporated into dust. She didn't want it, or anything else. She left the room without looking back, as if she were Lot's wife, but self-disciplined. We are now leaving the room that just a week ago looked old and maybe perfect, out of date, yes, but coherently so. Everything in that room has revealed itself to be rotten at the core.

What does that make us? It unmakes us. What we will become is uncertain, but history has broken like an old couch. Put it out for bulk pick-up and hope the removers are still working.

Note

Magda Szabó, *The Door*. Translated from the Hungarian by Len Rix. NYRB Classics. 1987; 2005.

April

4/3/20

Dear Patriotic American: do not ask what you can do for your country, ask what your country fails to do for you. "We're all at the helm now," a fellow walker says over his left shoulder as our dogs sniff at each other. Donne had his flea, we our virus. We are closer for being apart. The bank has blue tape to put our feet behind. I step aside to let two joggers by. This is not writer's block, because I can write just fine. An older woman pushes her walker around the block; she walks more quickly than we do, wheels clattering up hill. A self-stroller, she pushes the handlebar against loss of balance. Gravity is still in order, and the weather still fickle. Out back, a maintenance guy is mowing. Must be an essential service. "It's ok," Bryant says, "he's getting a paycheck." I remark to a tree trimmer that he's still working. His face lights up. Thank God. No longer looking for the quick connections, the inadvertent puns, the fertile typos. The mountains, Dōgen writes, are walking, and we are walking in them. We cannot see them walking because we live inside of them. The zoom conference gave us permission to speak our minds through tiles of tiny heads. Play twister with the squares on this screen. The neighbor with two Rottweilers and a black Dachshund has a chain link fence beside her concrete lanai. Between concrete and fence I spy dog toys. The spiky balls resemble COVID-19. CO meaning with. VID records image. Corona is the sun, the virus its stunted rays. The dog lost the sun and virus; to him they are invisible. But we see them with eyes of accident. Eyes that we're now advised to cover, along with our mouths and noses. Our ears are hooks, our noses off-set shelves. The brain is a carrier. The aircraft carrier's captain was fired for saying his soldiers didn't deserve to die of the virus. He did not go down with the ship; he walked down the gangway to a waiting car, then turned to wave to his men and women. His emails were unsecured. He called his sailors "assets." The asses have gotten too big to cover, though the president fully intends to keep golfing. We've rented the golf carts to let him play, and play.

4/6/20

A spectator's disciplined trauma, mediated by screens. Turn on, turn off: the president promises death, hisses its syllable into the mic. The surgeon general calls it Pearl Harbor. The governor refers to the apex. We need to flatten the curve, make a literal reading of the graph's symbolic ascent and fall. To a child, it might resemble a roller coaster. We learn to read pandemic. Someone said he was horrified that characters in old movies fail to practice social distancing.

I live beside the palm at the end of my lanai. It's like being in a poem, where I watch the thing before it clangs into metaphor. I watch a television that shows me trauma's edges. A doctor, a nurse, a family member, a friend. The patients are sicker than any patients he's ever seen.

Still a sharp blade pricks when another dog walker crosses the street to avoid me. My breath might contain death. I am but a carrier; the virus is agent, and we its subject. This sentence doesn't happen at once. I reconstruct cause from effect and keep walking the dog.

Age simplifies, mandates touch. I wanted to reach out at the moment abstraction imposed itself. If we're lucky, we live in thought. If we're essential, we cannot. To be essential is to be endangered. An essential thought stinks of diesel; it dissipates. Remember you are not important.

4/9/2020

Poems of Hope and Resilience. Some of us "have" time; others are "running out." She notes a bias against stasis in coronavirus reporting. All the sad stories of people leaving their houses, not of those trapped inside. The virus is a mountain that walks, that knows where the key spot is, that enters through a crack in the floor, a bloodshot eye, a nostril. Feel your breath, first in one and then the other channel of the nose. Follow it down to your throat, your pelvic bone, your knees and ankles.

The title presumes that poetry is a verb. A deliverable. Comes of a supply chain, diverted to the private sector, the one that owns the leisure to read. Those who are free to wear masks, do. Black men get kicked out of Walmart for wearing them; at least they usually get out alive. The mask distances us, but distance can be frightful. I cannot read faces, though I have time to shop for my essential goods. Essence = gasoline.

Light on the palm, mitigated by shadow lines. I hear voices past the range of droplets. My social media an invaded host. We used to call the meme *viral*. Some words translate better than others. "Given" all the time in the world, she can't write. This, she writes, is normal.

Flight is a seduction, and so is fight. The flight in a
poem comes not after fight but after bird-watching. We
see the bird, then we ask it to mean something more
than bird. So we go all transcendentalist and shit, see-
ing sky inside our brain and populating it with song.
Sun Ra on the roof, synthesizing.

After the fires, she said she'd lost her fight, then found it
again. After the plague, London burned. After a World
War, the Spanish flu. Disasters magnetize. He's doing a
great job, the best job, a sublime job.

More people out on the sidewalks, but fewer of them
talk. Choreography of avoidance, as the road is a tennis
court where we bounce back and forth, with or with-
out dog. There's yellow stripe to mark the absence of
net. I remember watching a spider on her net for hours
as she performed her deadly labor.

The net seduces, but breath abandons the body. It was
so hard to breathe, his boss told him. He has to log
every interaction he has with people, even at six feet
apart. Now they quarantine sailors before they sail, be-
cause everyone always gets sick at sea. The net brings
together what we do apart. The president begins his
presser with the wall.

Mask disguises emotion behind safety. You wear the
mask for others, not yourself. You don't tell them how
you are, but ask after them. When you take the mask

off, wash it in soapy water. *No soap!* the demented woman yelled. One disease kills off what the other disease hath wrought.

4/11/20

The question of grief. She argues the word is being misused. Did we not grieve for the 9/11 jumpers *before* they hit the ground? An edifice stands, but we see it shift, begin to fall. Those inside are still alive, but we've begun to lose them. This happens on repeat on the news. He said he watched the towers fall only once; I took that to mean he wasn't stained by repetition. Grief inflates, until it pops.

That's to get far away from the central facts. The virus kills thousands a day, but the president's tv ratings have gone up. His incompetence offers us relief from our grieving.

Define "immediate family." The immediate of time, or immediate of space, or immediate of blood or other kin. She loved her father but doesn't appear in his credits, as she was step-. He walked home one late night after a gig so she could buy shoes the next day. What we do for our later-to-be-erased loves.

Forgive us our daily nattering. Forgive the dog her bath in the sun, the cat his barf in the bowl, the other cat her pee on a blanket, and the other other cat his claws in the screen door. Forgive us our sins of omission. The faces of ER doctors look at us through bruises their masks made. A Sharpied date lets you know how many times the mask has been worn.

One doctor taped a photograph of himself on his jacket. All the dying man could see was a mask inside a mask inside a garbage bag.

4/13/20

Some of us have spiritual experiences. Others of us die.

4/14/20

A new SUV appears in a neighbor's stall, wearing a combat vet license plate. The property manager kicks rocks off the sidewalk. Torrential rains last night leave after-images of waterfalls. Nothing happens, a student says of *Midwinter Day*; it's just a lot of nothing. Another is jealous of Mayer's ordinary life: *her* life is injury.

Who did it? Radhika asks, on awakening. It's not that kind of show, we tell her; it's a mystery, but of a different kind. I, too, fell asleep. Did he escape? I ask. No, not in this episode, Bryant answers. The locked-in residents of nursing homes die without tally. He has flattened the curve by not counting them. A patient suffering psychosis understands the press conferences no better than we do.

Our neighbor is a cop; his dog needs surgery upon surgery. They'll do the surgeries for free, but the anesthesia is $750 a pop. She's had three already, and sometimes seven won't get it done. She pulls and pulls at her leash; she's strong, he says, though he has to water down her food. There is an end to this, but no one brings it up.

We'll all know someone who died of it. The mystery isn't who, but how it happens that we're taken. Touch of hand to hand exchanging money or a ticket. Breath on your neck in the subway. The jogger who goes sweating by. We aren't suspicious of each other so much as of each other's bodies, their excess breath, their unknowing.

If we're alive next year. That phrase requires a comma at the end, though we work toward the final period. Grammar holds, doesn't it? Or is death a new dialect we're learning to speak, noun by verb by declension? Who's got the possessive in this case; do we own our death, or it us, or is this not the question to ask? And of whom?

"You're not supposed to go into your patients' rooms and find them dead," a nurse said on television, weeping.

4/15/20

Things we can't do with our hands: shake them, touch our faces, leave them unwashed, pay without sanitizing, open mail without spiritual doubt. The provenance of everything is out of our hands. What our hands cannot reach they cannot infect. Second-hand is also suspect, especially when it's smoke.

Get a handle on your feelings. They've got swing, like a big band, but some days they strike out not for the territories but over home plate.

She must have been surprised when Igor Stravinsky dropped by to suggest she rewrite his Fire Bird. He appeared young, not the old man of the record jackets. He dropped by before the other gods, and Dvorak, whose music she reclaimed for field workers by way of Krishna. Asked how hard it was to be both black and homosexual, Baldwin laughed and said he thought he'd hit the jackpot. I remember his hand, the cigarette's trailing smoke.

It was the age in which everything was new, mandatory prefix to the old. We suspected that the new was more sound than substance, that fresh ways of thinking were being advertised like shampoos or skin care lotions. There is nothing but surface now, a friend writes. That's true, so long as we stay put. Pert.

Stay put is a double verb. Watch the menacing faces through glass of people protesting stay-at-home orders. To protest staying put they stay put in their pick-up trucks, blocking ambulances. It's a new amendment, the right to spray sputum on one's fellow citizens. The right to carry your viral load without a background check. Open carriers.

The virus as malevolent rhetoric. Breath exchanged. It used to be communication, now it's communicative. One more image of the virus and its spikes and she'll stop reading the newspaper. Almost as bad as graduation photos from the 1970s that are supposed to make our kids feel better about not having them. Image was anodyne; now it's care's antithesis.

It is not I who am suspect, but my bodily functions. Don't sneeze or cough dryly. It's my carrier that's guilty, like a car made responsible for a wreck after the driver falls asleep. A new containment policy, not against Soviets but the self. I keep myself away to protect your self. So who then protects me? The old tapes begin to run again.

The Alzheimer's home was always already a waiting room. "Get me out of this morgue!" her mother yelled, presciently. "When we get out, will we live together?" an old woman asked her lover on the couch. The same refrigerated container comes for you both.

Our work is watching. Watching screens, watching numbers climb, watching the parking stall next door, watching the press conferences. In her old age, my mother watched an empty street through her dining room window. Watching is surface attention. The screen is socially distanced and we're now at two carts' distance apart at the so-called Safeway. Do not attend services of any kind. In French the word is to assist. I will assist at your concert.

I can attest to that. Fewer being tested than last week. The curve flattens. Trucks carry Trump stickers. A mother carries her child. It can't be the same word.

4/20/20

The Chinese woman wearing a straw hat and black pants sings as she walks. An older couple stops at the curb to check their steps. Bryant chants "little roaches" as he kills them. They're social creatures, so he doesn't feel great. Birds skitter over a bass line of construction truck tires. Power tools or saxophone scales? So many musicians dying now.

A white woman leans out of a silver truck, clutching a sign about freedom. It's in the same font as all the others. A nurse in blue scrubs and a mask stands in the crosswalk, blocking her way. "Go back to China!" she yells. He's protecting the ambulance route into the hospital. *To* replaced *from* in our lexicon. We are free to infect each other. Funeral rites are difficult, what with social distancing. It's not the dead who scare us.

Hyper-focus on the mossy wall to spot a lizard. Zoom in on a leaf growing through a gap beside the lanai. Modulate your ear to listen for the shama thrush. This is not trauma but self-defense, this alertness to detail. We quarantine ourselves from the news some days; it's not healthy for us. Our respiratory systems cannot handle another press conference. A former colleague's partner is in the ICU with pneumonia.

I meditate with a group over zoom. The teacher says don't record the part where we only sit. A slight against silence, I think. The image of silence is still photograph. Lilith and I turned the corner to deposit her poop in green dumpster #3 and came face to face with a hobby horse. Wonder if they ever fixed the springs on those things, Bryant wonders. They sure could pinch your fingers.

Oil costs less than nothing now, at least on screen. My student says she reads Marx for fun, recommends a video on communism (if I have the time). The death of capital, foretold. Pundits keep wanting the president to act like a normal person. When asked, he says, "People love me. I won the election." He says "death" like it's uttered in foreplay. Cosplay president, dressed in a long pink tie, shuts the country against its "Invisible Enemy," which looks just like an immigrant. Brown.

Plasma thins, the circulatory system wobbles. A doctor says you can be breathing well one hour and require a ventilator the next. My mother's pulse was strong, even as her breathing stuttered. She scored high on abstract thinking when she forgot to eat.

I wake up with loss on my tongue, behind my eyes, in my bones. The old slide shows were quicker, but this one clicks, then stops, clicks then stops. The immigrant who ran a corner store in Chiswick gave me candy when I came back. The neighbor's dog, so cranky it ended up shipped to the pound after she died. The cop who told my son something wonderful would happen tomorrow. Loss is of a piece; that's its allure.

It's a collection of broken things, like pottery whose lines swirl and end at a jagged edge. It's feared because it's past: we lost loss. Sirens scream down the highway; a cop turned against the signal, with his blue light on. Later I saw him escort two older people out of the school grounds. They were talking story through their masks. Social media's a legacy site, where we grieve for friends we don't know of friends we hardly do. It's real grief, but.

Systems fall apart, like poems into prose, like buddies into monks. Some days it seems that to record the process is to succumb to it. Not process but actual collapse. She lost Wisconsin by several thousand votes, as hundreds of thousands of votes were suppressed. She should have campaigned more. Effect no longer correlates with cause. Time is rigged.

4/23/20

April is the cruelest National Poetry Month. An anthropologist quotes Eliot in his book about Cambodian farmers. "Raindrops keep falling on my head" played on a domestic flight from Phnom Penh to Siem Reap. Flying back, we nearly landed before the runway began. If you bought stock in words, they have little value now. One day he wants businesses to open; the next day he abhors that decision. Everything by proxy, save self-praise. A runway is for models; he gestures with his hands, replacing scientific models with curvy ones.

White supremacists wander the streets of the city bearing their arms, calling for freedom. The retching of the earth, the wretched among us. There's no e-vite for them to meet at Ellis Island, to be "brought" instead of "born." The American experiment was adoption but now they require blood-lines.

A neighbor's family got land in Pennsylvania because, as Hessians, they'd helped to win that war. They got more land after the next war. His immediate family were coal miners. The American dream goes under, where air is dust. Meat processing is another phrase for virus contagion. He scatters seed for his flock of doves.

Essential weed whackers trill. A neighbor complains about tall grass; it gets mowed. A little boy with Hawaiian grandpa rides a small Spiderman bike, blue and red with webbing in the front. They have a portrait of the Queen in their garage, and the old man a grand-daughter named La`i, or ti leaf. Our mailman works to the sound of Rush Limbaugh. The cracks are showing.

"Are you sure you want to discard recovered data?" Loss
as act, rather than arrival. They are dying in the ambu-
lances; they are dying in the corridors; they are dying
in their beds. No one to hold their hands. Some are dy-
ing by their own hands. Not trained to witness collapse
without tools to prop up beams, navigate dark passages,
fix the hard drives. Look into the middle of your brain
and install a light. Move the light to your heart. I see a
wavering candle, but it smells inappropriate, so I con-
centrate on only one nostril at a time. They say the swab
is painful. Perhaps so is the mask, given that our vice
president refused to wear his. The privilege of flouting
privilege. Killing machines have been privatized; immi-
grant labor does the essential work of providing us meat.
The mistake was to count their dead. On her walk she--
Jewish--passes the crematorium, sees and smells smoke.
Context is everything, my daughter tells me when she
doesn't get a joke. Contact comes of old context; one
woman says she hasn't touched another human being
in six weeks. *Isolato* is a significant word in American
literature. Or *isolate*, as noun. The contagious hospital
blossoms into meaning. We are given photographs of
brutal buildings with square windows; sometimes we
even get inside to see the nurses dance. It's the voices
that sound crushed, toneless, tuneless, a drone coming
out of the bardo's waiting room. As stylish as any wait-
ing room, this one is small, so only one person can sit
in it at a time. It smells of disinfectant, like the bank.
What we take out is not food or funds, but ourselves,
alone. Some doctors put photographs on their gowns,

because you cannot see their faces otherwise. The photograph will not hold your hand, but it smiles at you. His brother fought the system and allowed a man to die while on facetime with his family. It was some relief. The word is "closure," like a door or a curtain, but we don't know what we close in or out. "We will all need help," a Houston nurse says on her front porch. Her husband lets her know she survived the day, can keep counting down. Houston, we have a problem. One astronaut said he felt death in their capsule, though they made it to the blue Pacific. Astronauts and POWs came off planes with wobbles in their steps. Some things are better now, my neighbor says, because we're not driving. The earth is being cleansed. They want us back at work so we'll forget this time alone with our thoughts, breathing in the air. A weed whacker starts near my lanai, and I note that it was once upon a time a sign of progress. No need to pull a rake, or lean over. No need to touch the earth. Hear it sing, its gasoline engine and flailing wire. Watch the greenery explode in air. Do you want to watch another old baseball game, my son asks me, and we agree we'd prefer not to.

4/30/20

Open or closed: door, window, business, nation. Travel away from the literal and words begin to dissolve. She doesn't know what she thinks of the doctor's suicide staying in the news for four days, and I don't ask what she doesn't know. It's a feeling, I suppose, that some are privileged even after their dying. The Bronx EMT who shot himself garnered a half hour. That's what a cv will get you these days, the right to die on page one, repeatedly. Her father says she put on the harness and went to work. She was in the traces, but collapsed after her last shift, like an overworked animal. There was more about horses, too, a barnyard of them. An Iowa sheriff's voice cracks; the public health director stops to gather herself. To grieve publicly has no resonance beyond the news cycle. We grow jealous of those who cannot remember us, even our parents. When I ask my students about their feelings, they tell me they avoid the news. Do you know to stay inside? I ask, and they say yes. "Ignorance is bliss," one says from between headphones. The pressure of reality is registration for the Fall. I am of two minds: there's comfort in their small rooms, tucked away. Who would take that from them? Climate change renders trees in Minnesota unable to reproduce; the trees of upstate New York will need to migrate northward to survive. If we don't know a tree can't reproduce in a forest, does it fail or not? If we don't know "vulture" modifies "capitalism," are we not carrion? Do we evade ethics, if we simply never knew? The Israeli officer was liable because he forgot, not because he never knew. If meat workers aren't counted as sick, are they not well? The supply chain takes on new resonance. There's a chain around the monkey pod tree by the parking lot. Its roots wrecked the cement pad on which our mailboxes sit. So they're moving the boxes to the other side of the same tree. The other day, a neighbor said, they cut out a root the thickness of a large pipe. No wonder the monkeypods make such clatter on the road when they fall. The neighbor who tells us about the tree drinks Monkey Shoulder. It's whiskey. Meat workers are mostly immigrants, documented or not. By executive order, they will kill and be killed. They cannot be contained to the killing factory, because their roommates and friends are nurses, bank tellers, waiters. It's a chain of being, being chained to labor. An undocumented woman in Texas gave birth before she died of COVID-19. The hospital won't say anything about the baby. Someone's privacy might be violated.

May

5/2/20

His family's pain occurs somewhere between kindness and his inability to express it. My students are caught between a sense of foreboding and their refusal to look at it. Erica says we're in the liminal space now, a space where we can't write. But some of us fools do, because what is there to do but balance our thoughts against the weight of a crisis? The absurdity of it makes for a good topic sentence, though the transition flounders under a great weight of evidence. The man at the sentry box tells me to do my research, but when I ask where, he won't tell me. Somewhere on-line. All he knows is that he's right. But he doesn't care what I think because he knows I won't agree. Breakdown of culture diagnosed in the failure of sentences to cohere, to link phrases with any purpose other than performance. My own performance was too loud. I ask my students to write their final essay as a dialogue between writers we've read. Shall they pit Terrance Hayes against William Shakespeare, or is poetry still too fine a cloth to be dyed in stolid colors? One student used a Shakespearian English generator that promises not to be accurate. The new press secretary says she will not tell a lie, then tells a big one. One day, Trump says the states should open; 24 hours later, he says they should not. I need stronger words, not just the same ones uttered at higher pitch. "Hypocrisy" and "graft" are too tame, especially when one meant "actor" and the other creates better apples. But back to the ambiguities of kindness, the way it can show on a face but not in a body or its words. Self-isolated signals do not generate light. His being damaged still damages. Between intention and expression, a space that can't yet be crossed. His inabilities have been willed to us. But an inability to protect is not refusal. He was not the one who cannot be forgiven.

5/4/20

Post communication culture. I won't agree with him, so he says he doesn't care. As if his caring came only after right reception of what he calls his research. What is his caring to him? If I agree, he's corroborated. If not, he drops his affect, glares at me as I turn to walk away with my dog. In the Fascist Care Home, love is abridged only by difference. The more same you are, the more you are loved, so long as your same remains their same. Recite a pledge each morning to agree with the person who cares for you. Else your caregiver take herself away, move on to another patient. The music's not good any more, but the beat is sure, and there are lots of snare drums. Television testifies to old battles, those won by the good guys. If my caring means nothing to him, who then am I? I speak in words, sentences--try me on paragraphs--but they turn to dust before they get to him. It's the scene where you thought you'd found your twin, but in actual fact you'd found a mirror image of another kind. My student remembers childhood trauma on her walk. I suggest she describe only what she sees outside herself. It's maybe a half hour of relief, in the absence of care. So she watched as several men carried a fallen palm tree to the canal and pushed it in. I saw a cluster-spray of palm roots at Lanikai Beach yesterday; part of the tree had washed up. A little girl took its stage, holding her mother's hand, and looked at two large brown dogs walking the beach with a knock-kneed man. The beach was otherwise empty, except for two young white men who tossed their bikes down and walked into clear water. As I left, I saw a sticker on one bike: "A`ole Haole."

"But he *is* one," I said to a woman walking beside me. She sounded European, muttered to herself how good the water felt. A line of people stood on one of the bunkers, looking out to sea. The president feels a lot of pity, but only for himself. He says he's treated worse than Lincoln. I don't care. Do you?

5/7/20

America, I wake up wanting to vomit you from my gut.

America, I can no longer watch your snuff videos of Black men shot on the street for being.

America, I recoil against you seven times a day,

at the least.

America, I know the difference between contradictory assertions, nestled inside the cage of a single sentence.

America, if I were Moses, I'd find a body of water to divide and get the hell out of here.

America, the Pacific Ocean is too big; it's more than body, it's transcendent mass.

America, if I cannot part the waters, what part shall I take?

America, I abhor your children in cages, your citizens who want their hair cut, the pedicures an immigrant performs on you.

America, I hate your con jobs, your scams, your gas-lighting, your revisions of history, your attention to category.

America, I detest your gap between ordinary kindness and mass cruelty.

America, I hate your anger, and mine.

America, you are an instagram poet; your words look good, but I can only read them once before they melt.

America, you turn wine into brown water.

America, I hate the lead in your water, the lead in your children's mouths, the way you make the new dog flinch as if you're angry at him.

America, I hate the way you moralize work, then demand others die from it so you can eat your mother-fucking steaks.

America, you Moloch me, and him and her and us and them and all the pronouns that cannot put us together again.

America, I hate your love of guns, your love of spittle, your love of flags, of that fragile cloth that no longer binds wounds.

America, I hate that your cloth flags do not cover our mouths and noses.

America, I hate that you cause us to confuse the carrier with the carried, the pipe with the bomb.

America, I hate that you have volition and cannot turn away from your television realities, the petty jealousies that animate us.

America, I hate that I hate, that I can't think beyond a narrow wall of sound as it pushes us away from one another.

America, I hate that I must change the geometry of my walk to avoid my neighbors.

America, I hate that I think I know the truth, or at least some facts.

America, forgive us our trespasses, because we are dead set on owning property, mistranslated as propriety.

America, I hate the revolution, because I know what comes after.

America, I hate the lack of revolution, because I know what's happening now.

America, you will give us more suffering, and more, until we get the DT's or the TD's, until we cannot live inside our skins but exit into the ice to rip them off.

America, I hate the suburban pools, the pools of blood, the spools of the film that keeps repeating itself.

America, I saw the photograph of a man at a store wearing a KKK hood against the virus.

America, I saw a man shuffling down Kahekili in his slippers, gray hair matted, clothes unwashed, eyes to the sidewalk, construction trucks speeding to the north.

America, the malls are opening, the lines are forming.

America, I invite you to feed me, to cut my hair, to do my nails, and to tattoo my

back with a flag.

America.

5/9/20

The arbitrary earned, like forgiveness. You can go walk-
ing day after day, up the hill by the pet cemetery to the
power pole, hoping to miss the beehives beneath trees
on the trail, and you can forget why you so hated him.
Or her. Why the trail had seemed so certain the first
many times you followed it. Why you had refused to
look for bees, were stung and slipped down the path
slapping your legs, or why you stopped when you could
touch the mountain; these are questions that lead nei-
ther to easy answers nor to meditation. You stop look-
ing for answers, having misplaced even the question of
shame and guilt. She asked me if I knew the difference
and I realized I did not. Both build nests in the stom-
ach that resemble palm roots, smaller than you might
imagine, but complicated, like Medusa's snake-piece.
Embedded in the roots are shells. Settler colonists out
for an ocean ride, equally cast away on this beach at
this time, empty of tourists, if not of dogs. To imitate
Indigenous practices is not to appropriate them, but
to borrow them as a clarifying lens. She notes that the
sweet grasses grow out of the white and toxic sludge
of the lake. It's a kind of reverse toxicity, this bring-
ing back to life, the recumbent body of this place, its
breaths stretching ribs out until they seem less like cag-
es than open containers of air. We went to the meeting
in our small squares, bookcases and paintings behind
us, windows out and in. We had started to negotiate
again, from a position of weakness, bringing our chest
of modifiers, rather than knives, along to the picnic. If
you sit back to back in a meadow, you see more, so long

as you talk to the other person's back. The peripheral images dim, but everything else is stereoscope; two sides to the valley, two houses surrounded by rusted car hulks. A creek runs through it, twice. Only connect your clauses to complete the stream. A poet asks if I understand the term "free association." I do wish it were more like a guild or union.

5/11/20

To grieve, to air one's grievances, to grieve a layoff. To mourn, to feel distress. To be aggrieved. Take the word's quickening pulse. I asked my students how to find anger in someone's face; behind a mask, we might never be angry. The president doesn't wear a mask; he's all expression without cause, needing to be televised. I took down yesterday's meditation as too personal to another, even if the personal can't be contained in parking lot conversations or mutterings in grocery stores. Lines crossed, as if roads were all intersection. The prisoner always manages to escape but is thrust back in the village. There, he meets the woman he talked to the day before in London. A band of kazoos marches around the town center, as the show breaks for commercial. We're living in history, and history self-isolates, eating from cupboards, lining up when the food bank comes to the otherwise empty mall. The poetry of witness is easier to justify at second-hand. If a reporter tells a story, I follow without ethical inhibition. If she tells me her sorrows in our parking lot beside the green dumpster, I return my words to draft. Don't be grief's first taker, but take your place in line, six feet from the last source. If her story intersected yours, then tell yours, again. Echoes are the private rendered public. Take down what you had taken down. It's the verb that tells the story you'd otherwise take up. Directions were important to Hart Crane, walking back and forth upon the earth, launched from the bridge of a dentist's chair. A white woman in Silicon Valley crossed a small bridge in her SUV to confront a Black teen babysitter. The mother and her babysitter grieved together. It was not the first time. A young black man walked through a house under construction before a father and son shot him in cold blood. My mother used to do that, dreaming of a house's elusive mothering. She began to talk, late in life, about early trauma, but there was no talking back, to her or her childhood. Anger married grief, kept its vows. The compass needle comes to a point. The point is sharp, precise, locked within a marked circle. I carry her memories, breathe them out in public places. Contact tracing won't be easy.

5/13/20

The mountains, no matter that they walk, will outlast this human chaos.

5/14/20

Out of sorts. All sorts. Sort of that and sort of this. Machine for sorting votes. If we vote by mail, he'll lose, so he threatens the post office. Refers to tests as if they're pass or fail. Because failure is when you get sick and die. American at the extremest edge, but without any way to let go, go west, go and sort it all out. Endogenous depression responds to medication, but the tearing of the social fabric does not. At some point, it responds only to further tearing. Brian uses "tear" to mean a tear in the screen but also his name. We shed tears, then sort them in affect machines, little concerned at what they mean except distress. Distress is abstract, but so many students experience it. Where is it in your body? I ask my students, and they begin to catalogue their organs, the topography of their faces. You can make a graph with two hands, but there aren't any reference points, except air. That proves enough as gesture, but ill fits a works cited. All the bars in the state budget point down, a billion dollars down. He uses the word "it" to mean everything he cannot say, and cannot prove. "You know what it is," he tells the reporter. "It's been going on for years." It's a bad thing, apparently. Can a nation die of one man's jealousy and rage? Melany said the man with the one-eyed dog—Sangha never remembers which of them has one eye—yelled at her as she turned from Hui Kelu onto Hui Iwa. Anger. Sangha says he tries not to run into him, meaning in the car, and Radhika can't fathom the joke. Most jokes in our house are about not getting them. To get a joke is to laugh now, not later. We sat with Norman and Kathie and their unused amazon device, demanding that "she" tell us jokes. We laughed when Radhika did not. Bryant coaches her on the painting she made late last night of a mountain. It's not a specific mountain, but there's snow at the top. The man who teaches painting on youtube is wholesome, she says, because he talks about happy houses. Bryant asks me if all the keys are working, but he means on my laptop. Oh happy happy keys.

Her son told her that his mother was dead, and it was true. Who is she to correct the language of grief, unfinished? She wondered why no one was listening to her, why her words came back to her with "sender no longer at this address," why the president's whining suddenly struck a tiny chord. The photograph of the dog at the bottom of some stairs renders her as tiny bauble. Tiny bubbles. You can see ocean off the lanai through an opening in the palms where the mansions are. Bring us your rich, your housed, your gourmands. Lady Oligarchy's torch aims elsewhere. A man in Michigan wore a bazooka to the store, slung over his shoulder like a book bag. My mother burned a library during WWII it was so cold. My teachers keep saying that all we have is the present. His relatives, those who worked in factories, compartmentalized time until they lost the present tense. We're all living poets' time, our nets empty of birdsong. These meditations are intended to revise the past as it surfaces through bleached coral and a scrim of plastic trash. Accidental eruptions, Combray on credit. Revision not as ordering, but as manifold occurrence. The old memories come back as ours, embedded in someone else's history; that is how we know there was a world before us. Villagers in Cambodia do not frame their lives as episodes of violence; their narratives have more to do with interruptions in the crop cycles, with hunger. Many of them supported the regime that started again at Year Zero. One Zero crash-landed on Niihau after Pearl Harbor. A survivor overheard a man there talk about a sexual act with a three year old. Trauma's no direct path, not cause and effect but pain translated in the body as arthritis or the desire to drink. She talked about finding the rubble, softening the joints, sleeping without falling asleep. We fill our containers with murder videos, with hate speech, with open carry, then we assume our corpse position and wash it all away. It goes both ways in your blood, she says, and cleans it.

An economy of small pleasures requires lots of vampires and even more necks. I taught Melville's *Confidence Man* once in the 90s, mislaid my copy. The word "diddling" seems too kind, though our president's in search of one chair he cannot find. Echolocation might work, especially for a narcissist, but his voice dissipates in thin air. Nonsense means that it doesn't mean, which makes for a tough exegesis. Ex-Jesus on the road to Jerusalem on an ass. Brenda puts up a quote about needing to love what is unlovable, but the word *compassion* can't be confused with eros. The Kwan Yin statue up the hill sits at the end of a white plastic fence. She is the stone woman who gives birth beside sheer mountains. The tenants of the house are Kansas City Chiefs fans. At the museum, Kwan Yin is carved from wood, rests on a wooden platform gazing at a room of Buddhas. The conjunction of fast-rushing river water and stillness live in the walking mountains, sheer as corduroy, and just as riven. The president tells a farmer from Virginia there will be no one to guard his potatoes. There's a space force, but no battalion of potato protectors to ring the fields, save our starch. When I took the pink wax voodoo doll from St. John's Wood to a basement psychic in Bayswater, she told me it was real, made by "Blacks." Irish farmers place them on the boundaries of their fields, she told me, and her pliant sidekick nodded. Stillness quiets, or it disturbs. The dolls wear name tags, with form and function aligned. Kwan Yin has a name, but does not say it. He speaks the language of cure with nothing but words. Art may last forever, as Sonny Rollins says, but words get termite-eaten, fall in small piles of particle-board dust on our kitchen floor. I would invent new ones, if anyone would share, but we're a culture of self. (Whatever happened to that magazine?) If he wanted to play "Mary Had a Little Lamb," he memorized it. When he played, he had no idea what came next.

See yourself as you'd like to move in the world. My gray and white cat turns tight circles, front paws stretching out. Tail! He bathes one paw, flips again, falls, sniffs an open book, bathes, turns toward noise of rain and birds and circular saw. Pushes at another book, sniffs, returns to front left paw, hears cabinet door shut in kitchen, smells first book, props nose under it, sits up. Treatise on Stars braces like a lean-to on his shoulders, then falls forward as he returns to tail, bathes belly. From one square, a poet opined we're living in open time, almost in outer space time, floating. Who are we, then? Not the driver in the bus, nor the RN in ICU, nor the mourners we cannot see marching to a jazz beat. Not the talkers behind walls, breathers in ventilators, heart monitor beeps. Muffled breathing, muffled weeping, muffled dying. 95 thousand dead and no word. Words uttered are all lies. The truth is in our dying, our witnessing, our refusing to attend. The poet is a pall bearer, but he's caught in a video square looking out, lamenting a technical glitch that places him outside the screen's center. In an ill-lit room, a woman dances beneath a sheet, making and unmaking mushrooms. Not the mother of small children, not the student in her room on the computer, not even the cataloger of same. We cannot reach from square to square, so we wave as we would move in the world to embrace. We lean forward to read each other's names. We turn off the video so we can pee. It's a dance where we watch ourselves watching each other, imagining communities of squares. Yeehaw! One poet never arrives at his square. Let me turn you on. Or let me turn you off. But don't breathe the word *death* to the screen, for fear it might, like a stone, come into being as not.

5/22/20

Claude lies on two small black slippers this morning. Pushes paws into the slots where feet fit. Lies on one slipper, then flips on his back, grasps slipper to belly. Rubs his gray face on the slipper's bottom, then covers it, grabs the other slipper, performs a somersault, looks back toward the door where other cats sometimes skulk, returns to the slipper. Were the slippers not plastic, his embrace would kill them. Khmer Rouge cadres wore slippers made of old tires when they killed her father. Memory is a zoom background that slips in and out of a body. She filled her room with cells, kept losing her head to them. Bodies with cells on top. It's hard to do two things at once on the screen, though one poet read with only one eyebrow and half a furrow showing. Another poet's selfie featured migrant gray eyebrow hairs. The practice of aging requires discipline, an old woman schlepping across a desert. She focuses on anything that is not sand, demented landscape of cactus and rock outcropping. That's what shows as new, as most impermanent, what we identify as most like ourselves. "Change mind" was her first favorite phrase in English. Change mind is what her grandmother did, without meaning. We are, without meaning to be. Watch yourself as you want to be in the world. Then subtract reality from desire and want that, too.

I can't get away from the man in the park, the man
who sat planted like a mirrored C on a picnic bench,
back bent, chin to chest. I returned; he was gone, white
truck gone, blue lights gone. CLOSED reads the sign
on the swing set, held up with yellow tape. My daughter
kicks her soccer ball against a wall; an older man, drib-
bling, fakes out no one, stutter-stepping to the hoop.
Lilith reads scents on the concrete walk. In isolation,
we make causes to mimic effects. Or we get stuck on
causes, losing effects. I can't get away from the man
in the park. His isolation fails to mime a two person
game. He's effect without cause, cause without name.
His hurt is like the post-it note my cat attacks, before
he turns to bite his tail. "That's a heavy story," a friend
writes. Stories end when we arrive at their predicates,
but the ordinary stops short, like a woman leaning over
a cliff to count shades of blue in the English channel.
Her neighbor, who wears yellow pants, is an "alien"
from the sky where dolphins swim. I resist her narra-
tive, but admire the ending, love as sure as sonnets. "I'm
ok," he said. Words, aspiration, a flag to wave me off.

I turn away each time, but it keeps coming back. The white cop, the black man's head on the ground, police peering in a car, girl weeping who filmed the murder. I turn away, as if to turn my other cheek, but it's not my cheek to turn. My eyes see in not-seeing. "I loved my brother; why do I have to feel such pain?" There's acid in the cup that spills over in the street like tear gas, like smoke grenades, like milk that's use to cut the sting. She asks what the ordinary is now. An orchid pushing open on the lanai; a cop throwing a woman to the ground. Cat curled at my feet; empty clothes scattered on a sidewalk of shattered glass. Shama thrushes in the puakenikeni; "what's the use of sirens if that's all you hear?" Neighbors tell me to turn off my television; it doesn't concern your life, one adds. He's a good cop. My mother stopped our car on Fort Hunt Road, 50 some years ago, to ask a Black man in a stalled car if he needed help. "You *know* why that policeman drove by," she said to me, who did not. At five, I joked back and forth with one of the moving men, until I said in triumph, "you're a Negro!" What I knew already cannot be forgotten, no matter how often we delete our cell phone clips, turn off the sound, put ourselves under house arrest. You put the rest there, between the sharp and the flat notes. While grieving, Denise Riley notes, time stops for us. It's as if we're erased, but still move like we want to be in the world. And we do.

June

The dead man's brother breathes grief in, sucking air and expelling it through his mask. On the right, "I can't breathe"; on the left, "Justice." Everyone takes photos, even masked photographers as they take their knees, or chests. We take a knee, we bend it, we offer it. The officer's knee was a perversion, his blank face a mask with nothing on it. The dead man's brother kneels beside the curb where his brother died. He wears a Yankees cap, lives in Brooklyn. A minister lays reassuring hands on his back, his neck. Grief as the inversion of a particular violence. They are a peaceful family, he says. He loved this place; don't burn it down. The president hides in a bunker beneath the White House. There was a bicycle in the bonfire across the street. A white girl rushed out to kneel with a young black man. As the police advanced she put her body between him, their shields and batons. This is time sensitive, but not in exact chronology. Trauma's time makes an altered sense, like collage, except it keeps falling apart. Too humid for such glue. Elements don't cohere into proper equations, or chapters in a book. If you don't let us grieve our dead, we can't get six feet away. There are no ventilators on the streets to breathe for us. Americans refuse to mourn their bad history; this is the problem entire, a historian argues. I can't remember her name or her book. A man calls out "say his name!" and those in the circle filled with flowers and peace signs call it out. Breathe in his pain, breathe out love for the broken world he left behind. Watch his brother stand inside the circle, then exit its embrace.

Eating the first poisonous tomatoes of America—frightened on the dock. It's your 94th today, Allen; it was in her 94th year that my mother died, who remembered walking the docks of New York, watching war brides come off Liberty ships, noting their farm-girl incongruities with mothers-in-law dressed to the nines, who wandered the corridors of Arden Courts with such purpose until the falls and the pneumonia installed her in a comfy chair in front of a loud television, who'd begun dying nine years ago and kept on dying until the 14th of June. Someone came to the door and I said, "not now, my mother's dying." Her breath came in saccades, and then it stopped. She wasn't carrying her body but was held by it, and the bones of her thumbs stopped grazing across her narrow hands, every ounce of her energy devoting itself to the end of being. That is my path, a woman said after meditation; the slogan popped into her head. You came to Charlottesville, Allen, in the 1980s, installed yourself on stage in a comfy high-backed chair, a stack of books on a three-legged table beside you, maybe even a cup of tea, declaiming Pound's prosody while we gazed down from our wooden seats. Far from Naomi mad on her toilet, or my mother breathing hard on her single bed, far from her home on Lee Jackson Highway near the NRA, the road I never found on the first try. Your cake will be baked in the shape of the Pentagon, which can only be levitated with the help of financial advisers. Soldiers stood in formation across the Lincoln Memorial steps yesterday, row upon row of them like unlit candles, so

Lincoln couldn't get off his chair to protest his incarceration. *Only the flash of existence*, then tear gas rolls down avenues like a mighty stream.

Note

Quoted language from Allen Ginsberg's "Kaddish."

6/5/20

The point is not to capture an instant, arrest it, put it in cuffs and haul it to jail; nor is it to push it down to the sidewalk, watching it bleed from the head. Memory ought not be incarceration, but opening. The pronoun can't afford its abstraction; that was an old man pushed to the ground by a policeman. National Guard troops stand shoulder to shoulder in Lafayette Park, behind fences, shining beams of light at protesters on the other side, not to see them but not to be seen by them. There were slave auctions in that park. The incarcerated body remains not in the bronze of a statue, but behind the thin skin of a police line. You can fence out skin, but not the breath.

6/10/20

There was that time St. Francis used a suspect $20 to buy seed at the corner store. The guy behind the register called the cops, who arrived under cover of sirens. They blocked his exit, pulled out their handcuffs, fingered their batons. But they noted that St. Francis was a white saint, his skin tan from all of his do-goodery in the city parks. He drove a beat-up Fiat, but the inspection sticker was current. Someone had seen him cross the street, but he stayed inside the cross walk. His old ghetto blaster pumped out Gregorian chants, but not too loudly. Children loved them; a couple danced off to the side in the shade. The cops warned him about forgers, gave him his birdseed, and let him wander off to talk to pigeons and sparrows.

6/11/20

Make eye contact and small talk with strangers, Timothy Snyder writes. Lilith and I cross paths with the white man and his one-eyed tan dog. She's a small fluffy thing, dressed up in a large pink bow, and he's not looking at me. Rosie and Lilith sniff the important places, and I wish him a good day. He wishes me same. It's political telepathy: he knows and I know what we'd say, had we not the courage to go small. I wave to the man in the cemetery who thinks hospitals make money off ventilators; he asks after Lilith, who stepped on a bee, and I thank him for telling me the stinger was still in her paw. Death's tasteful industry spreads all around us. Gladiolas and torch ginger peek from graves' metal vases; a paper fish (for boys' day) lies on the pavement. Next to Kahekili, a bright blue face mask with white ear elastics sits on the green grass. Lilith walks over to sniff it and pee. ("We stopped for tea and gas.") Norman asks if we find a difference between our inner and outer lives; businessmen told him they hated their jobs more after the retreat. This is not who I am, or you were. Professions strip our spirit from our performances, as if we were good actors trapped in the bodies of bad. Hell, thy name is committee work. One man says he thinks any separation between inside and out is now false. I wonder how, without the huge chain link fence or the beautiful wall, to balance the video of a murder with what occurs in my mind. There's purpose in seeing, but less in re-seeing. Trauma isn't action, but re-action, stuck needle at 33 1/3. Jesus died in that groove. Trump is holding his racist rally in Tulsa. Symbolic action sucks.

Pull back on the lens. Mountains are too grand in their walking; point at the paper fish that blew off someone's grave. Then shoot.

Notes

Timothy Snyder, from *On Tyranny*, Tim Duggin Books, 2017.

Allen Ginsberg, "Wichita Vortex Sutra" also gets a quote.

6/12/20

The lotus bud is nearly as lovely as the blossom-to-be. Flowers, too, have their practice; our sunflower came out petal by petal, and none were yellow. The brown-orange flower winked at us, until it showed its full surprise at having opened. Its inner circle filled with bright dots, the outer like bird feathers, but no cape. The flower is not a royal plant, but ordinary. I like the dailiness of this work. The struggle to get inside the moment that hangs like water droplets on a brown railing after hard rain, to hear the petal's hinge as it opens, or the cat that scratches to get in, this is a poetics. Or a poem, and then another poem. I'm supposed to widen my focus, zooming back from a yellow dot on the flower's face to a garden of pots to mountains to island. But macro feels better at 61, like finding a droplet in the ocean, held fast by water pressure. The foam is either salt or detergent; you don't want to know because it scares you. Scab torn from skin, we see fresh blood beneath it. Everyone's freshly converted; long lines to pull on the rope around Stonewall Jackson's neck. The question of where in history we are, inside or outside or in the salt wound of it, means little. Little became X, escorted by cops from the scene of his assassination. We want our martyrs to be saints. The lives of the saints are in their absence.

6/17/20

Brush your teeth and just volunteer to stand in line to have your buttons pushed. I spread extra-whitening Sensodyne on my electric toothbrush, push the button and go. I'm careful to brush at the space between tooth and gum, to rest the brush in place over sore spots, to get at the very back of my mouth where the jaw clenches. The hum would be soothing, were it not so serviceable, like a leaf blower's muffled song. I rinse out the water, tinged with red, and move on to the floss. The line is not to be crossed but to stand in; I see someone coming toward me with her button-pushing finger out. She's angry with me, jostles to the head of her line, and jabs me with her index. The exercise is not to react, nor even to smile, but to stand with a soft gaze and breathe up the left nostril, and then the right. The breath makes circles; I'm as delighted as a child whose parent made smoke rings, expanding until they disappeared. Do I even breathe, the child wonders, if nothing's left but a smudge in the eye, itch in the nostrils? Go to the ocean and breathe it out, a friend advises; the salt heals, but not without a kick. It's the salt you gargle with when gums hurt. It's the taste of the spit in your own mouth. I tell the button pusher my name. The name bounces like a button on a rubber mat. Later, I'll take a closer look. It was an old button, from the days before velcro. Large and metallic, embossed with a cheap seal, I'll put it in my jewelry box and close the lid.

Note

Anam Thubten, *choosing compassion: how to be of benefit in a world that needs our love.* Shamballa, 2019.

6/20/20

It's West Ham versus the Wolves in our living room. The stadium's empty, cheering audible only to the television audience; players work in silence, or what passes for it in London Stadium, where we hear, or fail to hear, nothing. Here, a breeze comes in series through the rhapis palm, one frond a bright orange, the others dark green speckled with lighter green and brown. Seeds hang over the bottom lanai on octopus arms, if the octopus were green and its suckers small buttons. Earlier, I saw a white woman sit in the street in Tulsa, Oklahoma wearing a shirt that read "I can't breathe." She had a ticket to attend Trump's rally. Policemen dragged her to the sidewalk, put her hands in cuffs behind her back, pushed her gently into their cruiser. Then I took Lilith for her walk. The Buddha up the hill that's guarded by pink flamingos holds a rotting papaya this morning in his lotus flower lap. Back on the street, Kwan Yin sits in a black mask that falls from her face. She pushes it up until they ask her name, and she says Sheila Buck.

Take down the statues! Take down General Lee. Take down Stonewall Jackson. Take down JEB Stuart. (He stands in Richmond now with ropes around his neck, bleeding red paint, an orange traffic cone installed on the top of his head.) Take down Jefferson Davis! Take down the sad Confederate looking south, the monuments to imprisoned soldiers, to dead ones. Take them down with ropes, with hammers, with the heat of our rage. Leave them broken noses to pavement; let them breathe our history, smelling of carbon dioxide and blood. Melt them for poor artists to make no monuments of. But leave the horses! All over the south, they'd stand alone, locked mid-stride, always about to go to war but never arriving. Pull them off their pedestals and down to the ground of a park where children remember nothing but what remains as play equipment.

To grieve over what someone thinks of you is not self-pity. It's being on stage without knowing you're in a play. (This is easier in zoom times.) To speak one's lines offers a space for seeing yourself see yourself. But you're hardly the star, more an extra assigned to wave a sign, put in your 10K steps, then return home to pat yourself on the back. She worries that she's been shouting "Black Lives Matter!" for 20 minutes, but it seems to matter in a more difficult way when she passes two Black men standing on the stoop of a hostel. Her partner hisses at her to stop. To see yourself as others see you is a line in Ashbery; it's also a bad habit, especially when you don't know them. Let mirror dissolve into light, and watch light move up and down your spine like climbers on a wall. We climb for real on a fake rock face. But in a Berkeley park, a woman yelled at teens that they didn't belong there, climbing Indian Rock. She yelled the n-word at them. Her face is a mask, but no barrier against sickness. We turn our masks around so we can face them, staring through empty eye sockets and a mouth that grins through very few teeth. You've come to accept the mask as yours. Without it, you'd be too difficult to read.

Almost able to imagine myself alone without history in
the rain forest. This week's homework is to pray (knees
not needed) and to speak my gratitude. Feel grateful
for everything difficult, Thubten writes *Feel grateful
for everything difficult*, but an interlocutor in a zoom
box thinks that's also a white privilege. Feel love, Nor-
man instructs, while acknowledging it's most effective
for the lover, not the beloved. (To allow yourself to be
loved is perhaps the hardest part.) He reads a sentence
that begins with "perhaps," since there's no surety in this
practice, no insurance against impermanence. Another
woman in a box says she's lived with a doctor too long
to think anything lasts; she says she's vengeful because
that's how she was raised. Does she feel gratitude for
her vengefulness, or for knowing that it's hers? There's
room for warriors, even for tossing a man overboard,
but is there space for wishing COVID on the man who
mocks it? I'm getting away from my plot of rain forest,
the 9,000 square feet of no history (to me), from the
gratitude I feel for allowing myself to be loved, and for
the man who lets himself love me. A channel of light
pushes through the ti leaves, the hapu`u fern, the green
wooden beams that support the cottage. The light in
that tunnel soon fades, as rain starts up again, like a wa-
ter pump that's lost function in its air bladder, wheez-
ing and coughing when the toilet's flushed. I grew up in
one chaos and find myself in another. Politics is rhetor-
ical strategy, but rhetoric gives way to hammers. Each
word is sacred because it leaves the unmasked mouth in
search of an ear across the room. But if its only purpose

is to cuff that ear, what are words for then? Here in the forest, even words are damp, leaning over as in prayer like the fern fronds, toward the soft earth (layered upon lava rock). Ginsberg would levitate the Pentagon in his fever dreams. We choose to sit, to take exception to, to build a beltway around the heart. These days, everyone's speeding, but we remember the days of deep traffic, of waiting not for an open space, but for another closed one. The lid's been blown off now; there's an opening in the cloud. Dylan still uses the word "soul," perhaps because it rhymes with "knoll." The bell tolls and we end our meditations; history was flour sifting, but now it's baked in again. Save your crusts for the ducks, or don't, because that wrecks their diets. Consume the air-filled loaf, then pull the plug on desire. There's a census form on the table to be filled out. It will prove we're here in our cottage in the rain.

Is this word sacred, or that? That word or this? Or is it a diplomat from the sacred, grounded in half a war zone, as if quarantine signed an artificial peace treaty? Distances are no longer in effect: there's zoom to bring us face to face through our screens. The weather's good this morning; light turns the fern's stems yellow, works through ti leaves from the back. Light with no mirror still acts as one. Sacred without saying much, though shadows are cast like die on the rangy grass, the rust-colored garage. Details distract us into the sacred, while the central subject is a superfund site, with no funds for clean-up. Mirror logic: if millions are sick, take away their health care. In case of pandemic, stop the testing. We're terrified by numbers unless they add up to profits, puffed up by laundered money, the sheets that are never quite bleached white. (But white's the operative color.) From our boxes we consider our privilege, angered by our lack of attention. Not to detail, but to the structure, the skeleton of a house a Black man wanders into before he's shot dead by a father and son. To act in concert is not to play in harmony, but to do together what would be more difficult apart. Maybe. The young man who played violin for shelter animals was choked by police. Was that the story of the boy who threw a sandwich? Or the one with a play gun? Or the man with cigarettes? Or the boy with Skittles? Martyrdom turns banality into sacred places. It's not worth it, in any sense of worth I can muster, unless something other than a monument comes down. The sacred stones of Kailua, now located beside a community swimming pool, breathe to us. Our Indian friend says he knows what it means to hold a mountain sacred. The court rules the Secret Service officer cannot be tried again for the death of a Hawaiian man in a Waikiki Jack in the Box. Fresh off the plane, he felt threatened. Fresh off fragility mountain, we try to open our chests to what hurts us. Keep pulling. Nothing closes any more, except restaurants.

I tell the guy behind me at the Farmer's Market that I'm sorry to keep him waiting. No such thing as time, he responds, it's all a construct. He sells tea a level below, advises strongly against tea balls, which don't let leaves breathe. They come into the hospital, a nurse says, crying that they can't breathe. We tell them they'll get better, but they don't. He puts water and leaves in a big carafe and lets them sit overnight. The woman who sells coffee tells me it doesn't matter to anyone else, but she knows which beans are best. Her roaster is a 175 mile drive there and back; only open on Mondays and Tuesdays since the pandemic started. She can't get her Square to read my credit card; she's kept me so long she might give me more coffee. Time matters more when you can't breathe. The bio pic of Dōgen puts the slow in slow cinema; we watch him sit, and then he sits again. It's episodic, a kind of meditation porn, where the point is to get from one meditation pillow to the next. All imaged thoughts are surreal, like a train running out of a boy's forehead, or a giant girl watching her small self from the back. How to release them into an appropriate size and space. The girl thinks going over parallel bars might do it. I consider the violence it would take to free me from repetition. I saw myself drawn as a cartoon and then chopped to bits. Drop the name, someone said, so I did, and it resembled mine. The "conceit of deceit" is about thinking you have a self, Norman says. Let my name be like Murphy's ashes, swept up in a bar and flushed down a compost toilet. In due time, something will grow out of it.

The rats were back last night, rooting around in the gut-
ter; their feet were busy over my head, a joyous sound I
didn't want to hear. This morning, the brown cat came
by again, scooting into the garage when I opened the
front door. Light flickered on and off in a spider web;
was it the spider who pulsed like a lighthouse? A video
of thistle blossoms blowing on cement recalls an ele-
mentary school film of ping pong balls bouncing down
a road, except those had comical volition. The this-
tle blossoms begin a story; two meet on a lonely lot,
and come together for an instant, but then the story
dissolves. Buddhist stories never go anywhere except
through a trap door. The main events are interruptions;
distractions take the cake. A man waves his AR-15, a
woman her tiny pistol, at non-violent demonstrators
in St. Louis. They must only eat cake in that palace of
theirs; inside, there's a wooden hiding place from the
Reign of Terror. They bought it. Tragic history turned
to farce and then back, though they didn't shoot, as
there was nothing to protect beyond their ears and a
blade-perfect lawn. Go back and remove adjectives;
they represent attachment to a single interpretation. At
least pretend to detach from the Marie Antoinette sto-
ry, its reenactment in the American Midwest, updated
only in the citizens' attire (pink goes with pistol; khaki
with semi-automatic). Bryant tells me I liked the sec-
ond half of the movie less because there was more plot,
and I suspect he's right, except even simple actions can
strip it away. The boy on his bike, the girl on her parallel
bar; the story comes after the artist dies and passes on

a real ending to the actions he's drawn. The girl completes her turn on the bar and leaves the movie smiling. Yet nothing happened while they scrolled through the anime drawings, watching themselves being watched by grandfather found dead on the floor. As I walked to see the goats at the end of ʻIʻiwi Drive, a large-eyed boy zipped by on a bike. His parents said it was his first ride. When I came back, the boy had thrown his bike to the ground and screamed, frustrated by the hill. The arc of that narrative only repeats.

Note

Details from the film, *The Taste of Tea*. Directed by Katsuhito Ishii, 2004.

I have time on my hands, I say to myself, walking up
Volcano Road from the General Store. Does it reside
in my palms, or on the back of my hands; does it skate
across life lines or knuckle creases? Do we make time
by hand, or does it sit in the hand like a bird? The shad-
ows of hapu`u ferns on the road are like hands, and so
are the ferns themselves. I think about handing things
over, like my work, or my job, or my life. Put them in
the good hands of my children who use theirs to em-
brace our animals. I visit them on facetime, which is
a second hand presence. My students think 4'33" is a
rip-off; who would pay to sit as time passes? Taxes paid
for 8'46", and so did a human life. Put a timer on your
hate, and batteries will run out before the timer rings.
She'd known she was a serial killer inside, but not until
she stood next to the statue on retreat did she know
she was also the Virgin Mary. Radhika says Ted Bun-
dy went to her college and her friends all talk about
it. He didn't last long there, I might add, being a peri-
patetic killer, not a settled one. She refers to baseball
as "handy," because soccer is called "footy." It's handy
that, according to the press secretary, the President
reads. He's sore about his small hands, but not about
a bounty on American soldiers' heads. Hand to hand
combat gave way to IEDs; the actor reached his arm
into a statue devoted to Truth, and it came back with-
out the hand. Bryant called out "I'll fight you" from his
sleep. Muttered something about a newspaper. Turned
out the paper fought back, bleeding copiously, and was
as warm as my hand reaching out to comfort him. We

deliver newspapers with our hands, setting them in boxes or throwing them at stoops. My daily prayer will be, deliver us from this madness. But first I have to google today's date.

July

Close is the time when you will forget all things; and close, too, the time when all will forget you. Having lost the restaurant's name, I put out a call to recollection. Memory by committee works, eventually. It was the Garrett. A waiter gave me a free beer after Joaquin Andujar melted off the mound. One friend says the place was upstairs; I don't remember that. Another says he was there for Game 6, but I don't remember seeing him. Only John Lynch, kneeling on the floor, crucified by Bill Buckner's error. I remember basketball games, but not where I saw them. A psychologist told me John Dean had more confidence than good memory. You can't see the faces of Feds in camo in Portland. We identify the man with the broken hand by his NAVY sweatshirt; he approached them to talk, and one hit at him for the fences. "Marcus' period as emperor was dominated by confronting serious external threats to the boundaries and stability of the empire." Authoritarian regimes pull their border agents in to the central cities, Timothy Snyder writes. In the name of Jesus, a Black woman throws black paint on the yellow letters, BLM. A friend demands his family call him Jesus, and I wonder why they don't. John Lewis called his enemies "brother." What is most sacred is counter-intuitive. A little boy asked to touch the scar on his head and Lewis knelt to offer it.

Note

Marcus Aurelius, *Meditations.*

7/27/20

The calm before the storm became the calm beside the storm and the calm that came after it. It turned out we waited for the sake of waiting, organizing our deck chairs, pulling down the umbrella and glass table, exiling plants to the indoors, only to see Douglas pass 25 miles to the northeast. Duration goes both ways, either a cause for dithering or a cause that cannot be let go. Principle is (sometimes) the willingness to keep repeating oneself. They marched over the bridge three times; yesterday John Lewis's caisson crossed over red rose petals. Ritual's repetition designed to appease grief, let it out the door and down the marble stairs and back down Independence Avenue, or someone's avenue, past the Botanical Garden and the museums to another river crossed over by another bridge. Someone posts my words about forgetting on instagram; they're words I don't remember writing, emerging like a stunt double from the screen to push me out of it. As if to re-mind were to re-place an old thought with one that only sounds the same. It is not my mother who cannot remember me, but myself who cannot remember what passed through her mind when she'd been displaced. Not for another child, or relative, but for an empty space where no child had been. Reverse imagination, this erasure, taking colors down from a painting until the canvas remains like a yet-to-be advertised grave site or suburb. Radhika gets her reps in, navigating stunted orange and yellow cones ("Bumblebees 2009," one reads in her father's hand) across the field in back. It's move-ment, or the Movement, this stitching of feet across a

141

hard surface, dance of voices and billy clubs, the same struggle's eternal return. If you get old enough, you'll see the replay. In Portland, protesters turn leaf blowers on tear gas, push canisters away with hockey sticks, hold up garbage can covers as shields. A vet yells at unmarked Feds that he was a medic in Vietnam, where American soldiers killed 175 people in a trench. That was his oath, to defend his country. PTSD is memory's insistence, pepper sprayed.

7/28/20

The aggressor is a woman in a long black dress; a man in camo wrestles her to the street. He sticks his knee in her back while another man straddles her. The theater of rape as revenge is not actual rape, therefore cannot be tried. Because it's theater, it never happens. There'd been a Greek chorus, but its members turned away from tear gas and pepper spray. It was the year of not being able to breathe; hospitals filled with victims of violence or virus. Federal agents were silent as they roamed the streets. "Who are you?" a woman yelled, but they made no answer. Violence begins in silence. She'd sit in a room for days staring straight. She didn't want to say anything she'd regret, so she offered me her withholding. An angry quiet settled into the room. (Red and white squared upholstery, a file cabinet in the closet for important papers, hinged metal turtle on the desk to hold stamps, purple velvet inside its lid.) We gave you all the opportunities. The vice president's aide was sent to Texas to see kids in cages; her colleagues thought she'd feel compassion for them. "It didn't work," she announced, on her return. After a bout of coronavirus, she announced her pregnancy on twitter.

7/31/20

I have their ear and carry it with me. I whisper in it, ha-
rangue it, speak sweet nothings to it. When I walk my
dog, I take it with me, as open to the air as is her nose.
I put it in my pocket with a phone that keeps the time.
The ear knows we are grievable, the dog and I, that we
merit words spilled like water from a cemetery faucet.
(Take out the conditional, the active or passive verb,
this sentence's false engine.) The ear edits as it hears,
with an ear to rendering sound sleek, not clotted. No
judgment, just efficiency, the copy-editing beauty re-
quires to tune the fork. Not the efficiency of the pro-
duction line, but of the poetic line, which conveys no
goods, makes no profit, throws off its baggage like a
catastrophic alphabet. Lean over to pick up a lottery of
words and sounds, gather them in a baseball cap, pass
them around for others to put in order. Something will
come of it, if to come is to arrive at the ear's front porch.
Ambient sound is all sirens and weed whackers, tires on
Kahekili Highway and mowers on the field out back, of
palms and birds. As out of yesterday's television a cho-
rus of overcoming rolls through the living room and
out the louvers. If we have another's ear, if we feed it Al-
ice Coltrane, gently water it before the sun gets too hot,
we can caress it as it cries. Pull the plug and let sounds
circle, disappear (we hope) into a forgiving quiet.

August

What does it mean *not* to wear a mask, not to cover our delicate nostrils and mouth, our pointy or fleshy chins, cheeks bruised by the sun? A Midwestern couple checked out at Walmart in swastika masks, got themselves suspended for a year from shopping privileges. Ralph Cohen roared over his yellow jacket, "we don't know process, only product." Where do handkerchiefs come from, or lounge chairs, or even our newest cat, the flowers we never see but send to those who grieve? As a boy, he made lei alone. That way, no one could beat him up for his limp wrists and the secret aroma of a grandmother in the flowers. Trauma opens doors, but is hardly entrepreneurial. A mask will hide the mouth, if not silence it. We'll miss the cracked smile, the nun's dimple on her right cheek, the drama of the southern face. Read eyes instead, as you're now obliged to look in them. Louvers of the soul: turn a crank to make them smile or weep. A single mother cries in the shower; there's nowhere else to grieve. My mother refused to, except by proxy: a military man who died by suicide. "He was short, like Fred." That was not my father, but the loss performed as his, behind a mask that doubled as a handkerchief. At least there was a detour, once the dam was built. A friend grieves the murderer who was her student. But she knows better than to talk about it.

The girl with magic eyelashes loves her sister and her parents. Who is this person? they ask, wondering how eyelashes might make the eyes softer, and the mouth. The word "lash" has a history of violence and the preposition *out*. But her lashes perform another proposition: that to extend an awning over the eye invites the other in. Lashes are not a wall, because the light comes through. Sight migrates, crosses over a line that's marked so we think it's true. You wander out through striated fern shadows and plump hydrangeas to clear the retina of its rust. It's a trust exercise, this looking in each other's eyes, though one student said, "men don't do this," when I asked. Put your eyelids at half-mast, the teacher told me. There's a lash there, if only to hold us to our seats. A student, suspended for posting a photograph of a crowded school hallway—no masks—said she's making "good trouble." She's punished for what we see. She must be a real mirror, he said, if she sets off so many reactions in others. The mirror is an eye that doesn't see, though it shows. Tell me how this works, this exchange of self for other or itself, which is not exchange but a throw back to the pitcher. The assistant coach greeted his players with a Nazi salute, then apologized for his inadvertent expression of hatred. One of his relief pitchers pushed his right arm down to touch elbows, but he turned and re-saluted the empty stands. Nuremberg with no one there would not be Nuremberg, would it, but only a sign to take or steal on the next pitch? The problem with charisma is there's so little behind it. He's a poof of hair without a head, bloated body lacking spine, though body-shaming is not thought to be good form. What we see behind our lashes is either fast ball or curve. Another player tests positive. Another game postponed. We learn patience from our lack. The eyelashes last six months only. Time enough for quarantine.

An inner life of sadness meets its non-corresponding breeze through ferns and a tight corridor of light that runs across stairs and through horse tails. I turned to *The Nickel Boys* after months of procrastination. The handsome man in dreadlocks on the back cover is not the driver who picks us up when we're lost and deposits us back where we're abused and beaten. And so here I go again, headed down that road in my manual shifter car, angling for the shadows, listening for the screams. They called it "going for ice cream," which lives one or two notches past irony on the Richter scale. The other book begins in gossip and ends with a stalled love affair, a real one, the kind that sheds gossip for racial and spiritual allegory. In one book, the survivor starts a moving company (read that as emotional transfer); in the other, the survivor's a gym rat, a lake runner. Trauma's the crow bar that pries them open. A murder of crows makes offerings of gifts, rows of broken jewelry and awkward twigs sorted on a blanket by a human intelligence. To ferret out starts from animal but proceeds more like Columbo. We know whose crime it was, but we're more into the process of figuring out. Like re-watching a baseball game we saw before, so that suspense is in the art of the tag and not in the tag itself. George Floyd's image came up on the Brewers' scoreboard at the start of the truncated season. Silence for 8 minutes and 46 seconds, and then we went in to the ballgame, watching the empty stadium's blank regard. Kids set a Black Lives Matter table up the hill; the real estate agent from several courts down set hers across from them. All Lives Matter, her sign demanded. Behind her, a neighbor held a sign: "I bully fourth graders." There's a thin line between performance and violence.

Note

A meditation-review of Colson Whitehead's *The Nickel Boys* and Linda Norton's *Wite Out*.

8/13/20   —for Ninso

The hapu`u fern's sheath is dark, rooted toward the
bottom of the photograph; at its edges a layer of yellow
light blears through the fuzz. To the right a spider's
profile, outtake of the fern. Someone please tell her
the difference between allegory and analogy. Here
they might be fused at the fern's hip, quality of light
both retinal and conspiratorial. The perfect story is
written by QAnon, because nothing deviates from the
end. But the fern's not perfect, is story at the point of
translucence; nothing to know, the beauty of that fact.
It doesn't matter that you're not sincere in desiring
happiness for a difficult person; just keep doing it.
One day you'll walk out on the street and confront
that person with your own nugget of gold immaterial.
Hurricanes cross the central Pacific, only to be cut open
by wind shear. Their eyes lose shape and orbit, swirl out
into the circles Ninso's brush makes. He pulls it from a
Little Prince mug, then flicks his wrist. We get rain, but
not the full gaze of it. After being hit (again) by a pitch,
the hitter stepped out of the box and held out his right
hand. His index and third finger held an imaginary
baseball; he broke his wrist with it. This is how you
throw a slider that breaks, he yelled. It will miss me.
When you're attacked, do not attack back. Except the
hitting coach tackled him at first, when he got there.
Was he angered by the batter's condescension? Or was
it that "everyone's stressed out now," falling like pins
to the bowling ball you didn't realize you'd become?
I want to communicate with people somehow, she
says, but everyone turns their heads away. She waves

at her computer and we see her from our little boxes. Ticky tack. Suburban housewives live in scare quotes now; Trump confuses them with fear itself. White flight inverts itself like a cone. A tornado descends on Chicago, funnel cloud over the lake. If I were to paint that, it might resemble a transparent eyeball, nested in the backlit pulu.

A CVS card sticks between vine stem and tree trunk; there's a story there, of loss and partial recovery, but I can't tell it. In the Buddhist parable, a woman and a man bring their grand-child to a monk, accuse him of being her father. Monk takes child in for years, relinquishes her when the couple returns to apologize for believing the worst of him. It's just a story. Babies in stories are props, as are monks and grandparents. What we look for is the lesson, not the plot, no matter its sorrows. A child was given up by her mother, taken from her adoptive parents by the birth father, taken back from her father, and then? For the reader, the end of the story is its legal resolution. Your suffering in exchange for my wisdom is considered best, so I can practice equanimity in the face of it. The gun range is for practice, but what of the targets, their torn circles, their oft-pocked skin? When you consider the meaning of "abstraction," take into account its profits and losses. They're just stories, like the one I tell of my neighbor who turns into the parking lot to avoid me as I walk toward her, stories with no apparent plot to the one who's telling it, but clearly to the one who refuses to speak. Or the story about a tweet that made me into a character I hardly recognize, the better to hold me up as a "problem." It was just a story. I provided my name and URL and walked away. Whatever you do, don't look at the comment stream.

She plucks sticky twigs off other people's cars; picks fallen blossoms off the short grass; we walk our dogs at the same time most mornings. She's stopped talking to me, steers her dog into the parking lot when I approach, steps behind a tree out of my line of sight. I fear I've offended you, I said ten days ago, as she walked past. She didn't like the way I had talked to her the last time, she said, and I apologized to her back as she walked away. "Shunning—that primal form of human social organization based on the purity / pollution taboo split." Today I walk up the hill with Lilith, taking photos of red and orange arrows painted on the sidewalk, the words "ONE CALL," and a violet bush. I run into a man whose dog is named Murphy; the man has gray hair and wears a cap with the word "jazz" on it. "I can't wait until that orange glob is out of there," he says. Murphy loves the balls whose paths cannot be predicted. He chases them in the park by the swimming pool. Our neighbor in the Navy is losing his grandmother back east. They're giving her morphine, and she's talking again. That happens toward the end, I say, and he nods. He drank too much last night. A woman I argued politics with waves from across the road; her large brown dog stares at us. I can't think about depression and spirituality in poetry this morning, only about instances of encounter. It's a list without logic, a logic buried in examples that mask it. She almost said "mask" at the RNC, but used the word "facade" instead. The cemetery worker who called COVID a hoax now says it's real. He tells us not to put on our masks. His co-worker, who feeds the cats, said motorcycle accidents were classified as COVID to make money for hospitals. We wave, say good morning. Even when I try to write it straight, the stories tangle up. The closer to fiction you get, the more it's taken as fact, and fact has a bad name anyway. We may not be post rhetoric, but we're past its effects. Sound waves approach the shells that are our ears and fall apart. I see pieces of language on the sidewalk, catch particles of sound. You cannot be persuaded by broken poetry.

September

The aftermath of morning showers: an unseen drip, cold punctuation on my left shin, young birds screeching at older ones, a near-constant hum of tires on Kahekili. I'm not gathering paradise, but detail, to generate my sentences. A white ESPN commentator weeps because he can't imagine fearing for his sons when they leave the house. My laptop computer screen catches tears from the overhang. I'd rather be outside this morning where humidity is honest and light shifts with a cloud's white-blue edge. Is it unambitious to think these sentences change nothing, that it's wise for universities to cut liberal arts and train us into the high-paying tech jobs of the future? You have to be rich to write poetry, Lissa declares; the counter-economy still depends on a stock market to generate its unsaleable harvest. I go back to take out definite articles, as if they made each sentence rigid as Frost's satin cloth. Yesterday, each in his zoom box appeared worn; the teacher talked about love and trust, but everyone else talked about not talking about death. The trombone emitted not one but three sounds, a harmonics of blowing and singing at the same time. Each man on that Berlin stage is now dead. Sonny Rollins (90 years old today!) blows his horn on the stone stage just before he will fall, breaking his heel every time. Youtube's a fucking blessing, bringing back the voices of the dead and, as of yesterday, Lou Brock's stolen bases. The trombone with its pop-up slide makes Germanic jazz, and Brock reminds us of Jesse Owens. Memory over-determines history to organize events into pattern. Memory's a mode of counter-time, but it costs a Casio. A broken watch keeps no thyme, as my friend heard her doctor say. No thyme like the present, no pain that doesn't flower. I wipe tears from my monitor, as if my third finger were a rubber wiper and I a mother tending to her sick child. Each machine crashes in its own way; to each family its own unhappiness. One piece featured a Polish violinist playing jazz. It was a heavy, mournful, funny sound when the trombone laid its screech above the strings' low drone. A family friend sends his drone over a black sand beach in California. Nature can't escape surveillance culture. I do my best to evade admin's paperwork; have I listed my student learner outcomes, my foci, the Title IX paragraph? I don't tell anyone about my student "no show." There's money involved. That's another form of attending.

9/9/20

Insomnia's a generator, when the electricity's otherwise down. Hash and rehash, covid-bash, flash backward. The man who walks Murphy likes jazz, yes (it's on his cap), but he's been watching all twelve seasons of CHEERS. Yes, he watches Seth Markow (radio jazz DJ). I find abstractions in the cemetery; they don't begin that way but as cement covers, pieces of scrap metal, particles of petals outside a storm sewer. I tell my students not to start from truth, but to get us there somehow. I don't know what truths might be, and I'm pretty sure we never get to them, but that's not to say that the petal isn't worth our focus. Focalize, don't idolize. The closer you get, the less you're able to worship image or icon. Small Russian women singing. I tell him my ear is my strongest sense. It's not the image of the man falling on 9/11 that gets me, but the thudding of bodies on a roof. They don't play that audio any more. We still move to the deadbeat of our own drummer. The president tells a reporter he drinks the Kool-aid; I forgot that referred to Jonestown. Projection is a mask, and he wears it well. In the newer dentist's office I have to spit foam back into the blue cup I gargle from. The hygienist says the best place to fish is at Lanikai boat ramp. "The water boils in the morning with fish," she tells me through her blue mask (I catch most words, but not all of them). No more fishing Nanakuli side; great place to go but once you pull the papio out of the water, you have only a head on your hook; needle fish work from the other side, eating as you catch. One of the guys at the cemetery gate cheers as Lilith and I approach. I ask who's winning. The Raiders, he says grinning; they're beating the Panthers, the Carolina Panthers. We put trigger warnings on our poems for class. The bike shop moved, and the place now triggers him. Used to be a real estate office. Back in the corner behind the bikes is where he was abused. I get a forgiving comment about my Pidgin and google the author. He wrote *Why I Read Gertrude Stein*. The man who took my Stein class cries when he reads his poem about domestic abuse. The shotgun shattered when it met her body. His sister hid in a bathroom all night long. The actress said he tied her up and beat her. There's repetition, all right.

Two questions for today: is there a moral fiction, and
can the university be saved? We can't learn to dance
around these questions, as Dance may be on the chop-
ping block, along with Theater. They're cutting back on
performance, easier when we're all just heads in zoom
boxes, casting side-eye at ourselves. I can't take up space
in my box. I can't make myself a barricade outside the
next Board of Regents meeting. If I cry in my box, no
one notices, as there are walls between us. How can you
mend an invisible wall? Someone other than you con-
trols the "mute" button. I remember the Robert Frost
Motel, a small white building beside a minor highway
near East Running Brook, or was it West? Either direc-
tion is now monetized, with islands of inherent value
starved of students. If not enough students sign up for
poetry, then poetry dies. It's the new democracy; the
minority gets—at best—re-organized. Re-name reli-
gion as philosophy so it survives, but don't let anyone
major in it. The report says that students in religion
cannot get jobs. But prayer has been monetized for
centuries, and some institution reaps its rewards. Our
president is the Pope of IT. It depends on how you de-
fine IT, I suppose, but his vision is for a university that
trains workers of the future. It's hard to train the future,
but we're on it, because it's the rhetoric demanded by
the acknowledged legislators of Hawai`i. Think how
many students can get taught in their boxes, and how
few professors it will take to speak into them. Break-
out rooms promise liberation, but only re-organize the
cells. I come in like a drone, hovering over their conver-

sations until I'm assured they're having them, and then I hover on. I remember an essay about hovering in Romantic poetry; not drone, nor even bee, but a perfectly metaphorical hovering in place. Do you want cash for that, or will you check it at the door like your privilege?

How am I, indeed? Depends on how you define the word "I." Shaped like a cane, unbending like one, lean on it. I hold its top handle and lift it forward. You can't step on the same sidewalk twice. I read ONE CALL on this sidewalk, framed by red and orange arrows. A cop stands beside a trench; a workman walks toward us, his face hidden behind an oily American flag, his hands brown. Our new neighbor displays a flag behind the grill of his new jeep; a green line runs across it. He was wearing camo when I caught sight of him last night. He's inherited the Navy pilot's flag, hard to see down the stairs. The man up the hill who listens to devotional readings on his phone gave his neighbor kids Trump/Pence and Hawai`i state flags. He's an abuser, another neighbor tells me, though I do love his dog. My student disagrees with Toni Morrison that language can be violent. The flags are like affect, their effect pre-verbal, an electric shock. A Singapore artist took to walking through the streets in spontaneous resistance; when that became impossible, he played the videos of himself walking. Mediation dampens, but does not mute. It's the word that comes out when you try to type "meditation." Unmute yourself, we say to the inhabitant of one box whose mouth is moving without result. The flags are silent, but. It depends on what you mean by the word "kneel," whether obeisance or resistance. The first is patriotic, the second costs you a career. No one said anything about prayer, though Norman told us it doesn't matter whom you pray to. It's the prayer that matters. Does poetry have real world effects? Is this a trick question, they ask me, because of course it does!

October

They look at me askance: the neighbor, the guy at the cemetery; mothers with their masked kids at the play area. A Slovenian poet began from one short word, like *here*, then moved on to *elephants*. To play this game, you need a neutral word, one to which you can easily wish happiness. "They have always looked askance at the notion of western democracy," reads the free dictionary. I know "a" precedes "skance," but I want to hone in on the "ask." What is your ask? We're antsy to find out, like the detective show that's more about process than product. Show me your watch, then tell me how it works; neither glance has much to do with the time. Timelines are twigs off the old family tree. I saw branches in a parking lot this morning; at the ends that had broken off, the wood's face shone yellow. Behind its brow a coil of lichen, half-detached, lightly touching asphalt. It would be his own ass's fault if he died. The question of love comes up on social media. From our small squares we debate schadenfreude or forgiveness, glee or grace, as if we could pull them apart like splinters. The word "concerning" blossoms in our prose, having less to do with compassion than with worry. His vital signs do not concern us; they are concerning. Concern begins with a con, though it needn't end there. I say the Bodhisattva pushed one man overboard to save the rest, but my friends prove extremist. Love or bust, so bust it probably is. Clearly, Hope got her job on the strength of that bust. Time's expanded to fill space; we live on a giant soap bubble, roaring across a wide plain of water. Our bubble has nothing to do with cleanliness, but with a rainbow that stretches across its frail body, the flare of a palm frond in the sun, an amber alert.

The nation's a side effect: aggression, agitation, anxiety, blurred vision, irritability, mood changes, trouble thinking, speaking or walking, troubled breathing at rest. Side effects are character actors; they're loud and shine the light of their skin through the kliegs. *Nie mehr Krieg* was scrawled across a building in Munich, near the packed McDonald's where I took myself out of the rain. My mother told me lamps were made of skin and I tried to imagine how. It was as hard to see as sex. She had a light spoon with a swastika on it, kept with her other spoons. We never seemed to use it, but it was always there inside the drawer. Her brother had given her a lamp; the shade spooked me, as did all the others. Made of synthetic flesh, the shades proved translucent, like x-rays of a history she knew but I did not. We're turning the corner, the president tells us, but corner nests so close to coroner I can't believe him. It comes around, like the woman on the mountain, like a theory of history that counts only its repetitions. At some point, detail is both fine and abstract, as if the thing were the law that made it so. My neighbor leans to pick up plumeria blossoms under the tree; many have fallen on their petal backs, gazing up from weed-whacked grass, visible after divorce from the tree's branches. Beneath the controlled art, a scattered one. More out of whack is this: "I love that man; I would die for that man; that man is my hero!" They're not citizens, but fans. The star drives by, his eyes peering over a black mask. It's a crazy ball, but we're invited to come again.

The balls of his eyes are marbles, reflecting nothing but thick glass.

10/7/20

If we have not seen the president for 48 hours, does he still exist? The secret for taking good photos is to hone in until context is gone. Get so close object dissolves into detail. The lotus appears as many eyes on a flat green surface. Word scraps gaze from nests of grass and seed pods. But the missing president lacks even the context of a balcony. His allusions are illusion, his salute to none but the cameras he knows point at him. He returns for a retake, without sharp intakes of breath. If we have not seen the president for 48 hours, do we exist in the same way, as lenses to his skin, his hair, his tie? See how the poet removes herself from the poem and offers up a camera lens, I tell my students. It's as if the poet's on a rail at a football game, running back and forth like a wide receiver without a route. Soon the camera on a rail will give way to a drone, so even machines will be unemployed. To be redundant is to say it all again, without the force of a poem's repetitions. Redundancy is the weak strongman of rhetoric, divorced from a refrain. To write the poem of this time is to acknowledge one's lack of power. Words with power are told as lies, after all. To write the poem is to be stubborn, habitual. This is it, the poem, because I write it in the morning. When someone asked about the phrase "this is it," I thought he referred to Thich Nat Hanh. "I guess this is it" were my father's dying words. Thay is dying, though you can order his calligraphy on-line. Attend to the words no one wants, like "this" and "that" and "there." That's the poet's gift, dying into words that merely point. There's no sentence here.

November

The wicked witch gives the broom to someone else to
fly on. He's got Air Force One, and he knows how to
use it. America likes a boot in the face, a boot with a
warhead for a toe. I'm reading Epictetus for his wis-
dom. I hear him sweeping in the corner, the one I never
get to, and finding clarity in the angle. Even wisdom lit-
erature has limits, for who's to sweep behind the corner,
in the other unit, where the neighbor lives who refuses
to look at me. Ah, the gaze. She looks at dog, at tree, at
fallen petals, at the sticks that fall on car windshield.
Her dog looks at us, and I at her, but the connection
fails like an old modem, most impersonal of hang ups.
It's more mystery than hurt, months into the game of
hide and go hide some more. Like I wish I could google
these non-encounters and find some wisdom in them,
except I suspect there is none. The shift from seeking
meaning to accepting it—or its lack--has proved awk-
ward. Over the course of a lifetime, one study showed,
our personalities change completely. At 77 we wouldn't
recognize our 14 year old selves. But it seems quicker
than that, the metal screen slamming shut on ambition,
on accumulation of credits. Accretion's no longer the
ode, but decrease. Is it in the age, or in the meds? The
miserable reflection of a leader who craves suffering to
feel himself breathe? My students looked in the mirror
and saw themselves as functions: daughter, grand-child,
sister, except for the adopted woman, who saw only her
nose. I asked what it might mean to separate identity
from self. If the mirror is a thing in itself, what does it
ask of us? To touch that surface, like a faithful reader,

and know how little is left on it of us, save thumbprint
or a sponge's smear. An almost language, that. As we
step away from it, it fills with another self: bed or cur-
tains or a desk.

He takes photographs of shadows on curtains. Shadows need light to grow, before descending into dark. My students refer to their identities as wholes, but mainly because they so acutely feel the holes. There's a hole in the text, the German academic intoned, and he made a big career of that. Another student did an erasure poem of "Mending Wall," but kept the word "gaps" in. Called it "Mending All," as in "all lives matter," though to say that means they don't. The president hopes for Nuremberg but gets only a minor league park's worth of fans. He drives through their unmasked faces on his way to golf in Sterling, the exurb not the castle. The new mask is the lack of one; hatred shows on faces better when you can see a nose and mouth, the creases they forge in cold skin. This genocide is self-, suicide by other means, since many selves are pro-life. We think we're giving our lives, but they're being taken. At the Tomb of the Unknown Soldier, Trump sways back and forth like a kid who needs to pee. It's harder to find unknowns now that there's DNA on top of teeth, but we can imagine the unknown when we close our eyes. The whistleblower got a letter from the Defense Secretary who outed him, demanding his future silence. We heard about it. Silence is the unknown of speech. We choose not to say, or we are chosen for. He's firing people again. Only some of us still distinguish between reality and the show, the show and whatever inspired it. There were no great women chess players in the 60s, so someone had to invent one. Another magical orphan, lacerated into drink and pills, for whom the checkered board suffices.

Ça y est I could hear, but not spell. Sigh yay, was what I caught, like a mysterious man outside the window, hunting butterflies. This year trees vibrate and hum with bees again. I met a woman in the cemetery who lamented those who live there cannot see the view. It's for their families, I say, and she hopes they come to see the Ko`olau. I find a marker to a couple that is clearly still alive; their photograph is to the side, and they're smiling. The man shares my birthday, though he's five years younger than I. I'm reading a book about dying. It's a discipline, but you can travel there, even now.

Ding dong! Don't ask, it tolls for thee. Dying is a transition, long denied. I AM NOT DYING, he yells. As I lay not dying, I imagined the power of a deathbed on which there was no death, just endless waiting. The pings of machines matched, in miniature, civil defense sirens, and the boy who played "A Love Supreme" to mirror them. When is a mirror also vehicle for sound? The lake's face broke into splinters, leaving the barest asemics for us to puzzle at. I looked it up, after posting a photograph of a palm trunk from close range. Resembles words or tangles and plaques to no ambition we can recall. The shape of no meaning is as lovely as that of a line of verse, the arc of whose words you misplace. In translation, you choose either to convey meaning (with unionized labor) or to engage with the play of a broken belt, flinging its conveyances like a gorilla in a suitcase commercial (labor anarchized). The deathbed's a conveyor belt, from which souls are sorted and packaged for later consumption. I said "soul" does not violate separation of church and state, because souls exist without knuckling under to icons or strangers. The toy that grinned at me from the gutter surely a sign of something, if only of laughter, contextualized by chance. My death shall convey me, whether or not I deny it. She refused to cry when my father died, and so began my fascination with rituals of release. Catch and release grief: it keeps the ecosystem stable. She tottered into tangles, refusing a rebirth of grief postpartum. Bryant tells me the witch's green make-up burned, so Oz wasn't without pain. You mean it all happened because she hit her head? our daughter asks. Dreams look better in technicolor, and the red of her ruby shoes shows better outside the television. She was young then, but never grew old. She's caught in time, but only if we keep pushing the remote.

I put masks on my memories. What was said to me no longer has a mouth. I can't lip read, push my left ear toward a muffled sequence of words I know to be a sentence. If the sentence is an A-frame, I can imagine its sharp attic, the crazy slope of its predicate. Our predicament recasts history as social distance, a line you stand in, feet planted firmly in their icon toes. You in the frozen food aisle, and I in the Hispanic. Both of us peering at the beer cans. If can can. If no can no can. A page on which everything's erased except the punctuation. You'd never know it had been a sex poem, now that it's stripped of all flesh but commas and brackets. An exclamation! Consider what these forms of punctuation mean apart from words, or what a page of pronouns signifies without verbs or nouns. A detective novel written to find out who removed the sounds, left only pauses and digressions. How can I compose my memoir as a writer, if I don't think of myself as one? Art is excess, a flower in the cap that requires nothing more than to cover the crown of the head. We do not need what cannot feed us. I will feast from now on on warships and submarines, cooked in their own nuclear stew. A wart grows on my left little finger's knuckle, sensitive when I reach into a bag of cat food. It's the knuckle's hat or mask, a covering like black print on paper. What shall I read, now that I've finished the book about my last year? Learning to read is about taking off the mask, unshackling thought from type from word from breath. Anti-maskers make the best readers. My student zooming from his car in Reno says he dropped

Ben Jonson because he couldn't figure out what it had to do with job loss. I want to say everything, but not now. An Iranian nuclear scientist was killed yesterday. Who done it? We done it! That's call and response, I say to Radhika. Pilgrims get such bad press this week. (Losers and suckers.) The dog's collar resembled RBG's symbol of dissent. I teach creative writing as a form of resistance. No one buys that line.

From the empire of bad passes to the exurbs of yellow cards—groves of autumn trees—our goals stay put until the day we wake up to a blurry sun, having shed ambitions like jerseys, wandering into the streets of Manchester or Sheffield, nostalgic for pre-industrial fields we never saw but through the scrim of chimneys or an imitative pitch. Metaphor at the center of the latest twitter war, as if. We can make hills out of holes any day we please. "Sue fell in the hole!" someone yelled when I felt the canoe on my shoulders hit the ground. When she looked in the mirror, she saw her mother-in-law. The man on a horse called for a pogrom against family resemblances. The friend who pulled my Tarot cards found several knights of various qualities. The contradiction's not in the card but in the cave of the heart, distinguished from the hole by its rhythmic embrace. Blood relations spilled, the picker-upper a sheaf of paperwork and a notary behind plexiglass to affirm your signature; your handedness puts you in a different family, one that includes the girl tortured for five years into writing right. If torture is an opera, then what's a string section doing out on the street beneath the stars (those that appear in too many poems) rubbing their bows across tunes of influence? When your music assimilates to standard, then you've lost it. The ref steps in to give you time on the pitch to heal your twisted ankle. Pitch transferred to another sport before it turned to tar sands, a poet tried in a court of law for blocking the pipeline with his words. The question of activism intrudes; what can this poem effect in the world when our factories of art are shutting down, their chimneys cleansed of performance? One knight's a messenger of creativity, but what are the stations of his cross? When he returned from a Christmas bombing raid, he landed on one. It was runway, not hedgerow, a constructed symbol rising out of the Pacific night. We flew over southern Japan, an illuminated text of water and island; you could almost play it on a flute, if you knew the notes. I bought Bryant a tin whistle at the Cork Airport as I talked to a man in a fedora. Days previous, he'd been Tom Raworth vacuuming a floor at dawn, mint julep in his left hand. Someone at the hostel said he came from the Taliban.

If I am one self on facebook and another on instagram, then who am I on twitter? And am I to myself who I am to my audience? On Proust's twitter I read the problem of happiness can be solved only by desiring less. Marcel and Marcus Aurelius walk into a bar, but neither is inclined to be in a joke, so they sit quietly and take it. Wisdom literature is as redundant as a London taxi driver in the pandemic; even sentence structures come up against the sign for repeat, two dots denoting a wall, at least for now. A boundary is always abstract, yet lives inside our bodies. Is it we who mend the wall, or the wall that mends us? Is mending what's at stake? Ask most obvious questions only. The answers will astonish you. Someone has put up a large painting of the holy family on their fence; what I notice are the fat fingers around the body of an adult baby. It's so awkward as to command faith, or at least drive skepticism in that direction. Joseph has his other arm around Mary. Was she cheating on God? My daughter uses the word "immaculate" in the English soccer sense, denoting a perfect pass. "Let it Be" came in a dream; Macca's a great rememberer. I dreamed that all the lots in Volcano were cleared of hapu`u and `ohi`a, even the invasive ginger that punctuates green with red. Make transitions using colors, or the metaphor of a forest. Then ask to go back like a filmstrip in reverse, tree after tree re-membering itself. They communicate, you know, suffer tree nostalgia, share recipes for sap, warn others of drought conditions, lend a root. Socialists, you know, these tall and silent types. Uncanny as Kwan Yin, who's seated just beyond a vinyl fence up the street. Does the renter take up the owner's faith, knowing it bounded by a lease?

December

Don't admire me for having survived the Unnameable Event. Listen to the tremor in my voice, but know it as symptom of the Other Thing I'm not telling you. Hear out my secrets, those I keep to myself, and watch my affect as performance. A young man tells you nothing, though he shares a house with you. You worry that he might rehearse a two-years-ago spiral, while feeling that you need to let your lenses down. The softness of bad vision is sometimes preferable to the clarity of hindsight. Don't ask questions, because they inspire more not-answers. She saw the sunrise from grandma's, though she doesn't say what it means to her. My letters were sheer projections onto the landscape of London, circa 1980, though I felt that I felt them, so why didn't she? To give care to one who had withheld it is like scouting a route you've already stepped on, while wanting to bushwhack the rest. The road is the habit, and that's a bad pun, as my mother said, in her bun. If the Unnameable Event is communal, do you share it, or cock your head and say "da kine"? He'd lost nine members of his family in the blue building located between the place his father was killed and the restaurant where we ate in Battambong. Admiration's too simple a word for my response to him. What's wrong with finding the sacred in a man who laughs? If memory is habit, then be a slob, hoard so many hurts you can't ever find the one that hurts the most. Don't like hierarchies? Go for the social history of pain, the wounds that afflict the least among us, not celebrities, though god knows they hurt, too, on either side of fame's mirror. The Unnameable

Event, once spoken of, can be released like mouse in a field. Our affect, upon release, raises us like the balloon in which a neighbor's inflatable Santa rises at nightfall. Hot air makes him generous. Our speech shall make us admirable, though that is Not the Word.

Note

In response to "a philosopher and a professor" in the *New York Times*, 11/30/20

Make stark distinctions only, the better to knock one
down like an egg from a wall, or a wall in a strong wind.
If reparations come in the guise of prizes, then what to
do with runners-up? In England, they're called ladders,
the runs on stockings. Our stocking suffers from a hole
in its large toe, the one that stands in for five of them.
Five makes a team in basketball, so long as they're tall.
All numbers are magical. He tells me he won't take the
vaccine, because no one knows the side-effects yet; his
mother won't until she's assured no aborted babies were
used to make it. It should be his choice, he says, and
besides, things are pretty good here. If he lived on the
mainland, he might. Fundamentalist ethics are as rela-
tive as any. We guard our relatives least, because at least
we'll be loving them to death. Thank you, she writes of
her uncle's beautiful dying. I saw a green canvas cov-
er attached to a metal frame around a vacant hole in
the cemetery. Seven in one year. Family comes to sit in
folding chairs at graves neatly marked by tiny picket
fences. One man said the Lord brought us a beautiful
day. The brightest light in months, mountains a jagged
line across the azure sky, framed by Lilith's ears. More
talk here of paving the green spaces. They get torn up
in the rainy season, that of mud wasps and scars. As-
phalt's more permanent, scab without a wound burst-
ing at each turn of the cart. 300,000 in, he golfs. Pardon
is what pardon does. "It was disgusting, and I'm from
New Jersey," the ex-governor says of the president's son-
in-law's father. All within the law. The cemetery worker
asked me if I'd read the Constitution, and I said yes. We

shake our heads about the fresh grave up the hill. Dharma blossoms turning. When I said I'd taken photos of her purple flower in a pot full of water and algae, Judy said, "but it wasn't fully out yet."

It's the pronouns that terrify. Lodged between the pronoun that signifies a known quantity and the pronoun that's merely arbitrary, one pronoun took a gap year. Having planned to travel the continent, this she or he stays home, inhabiting the deep grammar of pandemic. Her poem enacted the loss of letters, until it became the page it was (not) printed on. He lost so many friends that he ate a large plate of mini-muffins bought at Costco. Binge grieving takes in more than it can swallow. Birds bring us happiness, but they also sing now. I listened to them on-line, but couldn't pull song apart from song; the birds blended, leaving odes in short supply. "Bird thou never wert" gives the metaphor shell game away. Buy the plastic shroud for the Fit, place it over the electronics behind the mirror, then push the button to adjust what appears closer there. Car parts, tree branches, broken windows, and the echo of an artificial voice counting down. We don't call this terror, but "a not accidental explosion." We meant to vacate our monkey minds, but instead find the Melting Pot shattered, its staff out of work. Terror is imagination made literal. "It was like a movie," the man said, his windows blown out. And sometimes Hollywood is like real life. Back to the shroud: it either bears witness to the oils on Christ's skin or to grief's gray hoodie. On the day of Premier League, it's a bonnet, mask lifted to forehead and skull, leaving transmission possible through the breath. We can breathe, but a foot's on the neck, all the same. "They know not what they do," can be said of many, whose logic struts like baby goats in pajamas.

Not knowing offers reason to refrain from judgment. In the dying days of this administration, more Black men are executed, more White men pardoned for their crimes. He governs by fiat. The blue car wears pink eyelashes over its headlights. What they signify isn't clear, but we're grateful that they're there. Banality is not evil, though it sometimes plays it on tv.

12/29/20

There are two oranges in the Buddha's lap this morning. The hoarder's yard is framed by Buddha and six pink flamingos, legs nearly lost amid flowers and plastic buckets. In Charlottesville, two men walked past a shop with pink flamingos in the window, each carrying a pink flamingo unrelated to the others. The movie (1972) was part of a "Trash Trilogy," I read, but then my internet falters so I can't retrieve the plot. My husband's name was Waters, until he changed it. By the waters of Leman the poet wept. One student hated him on principle, because he was a gatekeeper. We are stakeholders in the new dispensation, one that veers in and out of cliché, like so much, bearing the promise of something new but tangled in a net sack like an octopus. Use for bait, the fisherman says. Use for bait, my son says. Did the octopus look forward to seeing the philosopher as much as he did her? Do they wonder at our lack of suction, the way we stick to things in our heads, but let them go from our hands? How do we define ourselves without attachment? "I cannot believe I'm living in this time," a neighbor tells me. They are all around us, and they are kind. The women who suffered violence supported him because they wanted to be safe, and he promised a lock (and a stock and a barrel). The woman who interviewed them had to stop because she broke her vow of non-judgment. There was nothing to say to the nurse who cared for a refugee and voted for Trump. Ethics writ small. When you pull the image closer to yourself, it blurs, losing the pixels that defined it. Unpinch it with your fingers, let it travel away from you like a peg on a google map. For an instant you see nothing, but your body assumes its vertigo like a lighthouse where two men prepare to kill each other for loneliness. I ask him to turn the tv off when I see the rerun image of a man dying beneath another man's boot. Reality snuff shows keep us all in line, through the extremity of our feeling, which is never kind. "What's it matter to you?"

About the Author

Susan M. Schultz is author of *Dementia Blog; "She's Welcome to Her Disease": Dementia Blog, Vol.2*; several volumes of *Memory Cards; I Want to Write an Honest Sentence; Lilith Walks,* and the critical book; *A Poetics of Impasse in Modern and Contemporary American Poetry*. She founded Tinfish Press in 1995 and was its editor for over 20 years. She lives in Hawai`i with her husband, three cats and a dog, and is a life-long fan of the St. Louis Cardinals.

www.ingramcontent.com/pod-product-compliance
Lightning Source LLC
Chambersburg PA
CBHW020245130626
46549CB00005B/2075